No Trace of Christmas?

No Trace of Christmas?

Discovering Advent in the Old Testament

Christoph Dohmen

Translated by Linda M. Maloney

A Liturgical Press Book

THE LITURGICAL PRESS
Collegeville, Minnesota

www.litpress.org

Cover design by Ann Blattner. Cover illustration: © Sieger Köder, "Bethlehem-Efrata, aus dir wird einer hervorgehen," Wasseralfinger Altar (section).

Originally published as *Von Weihnachten keine Spur? Adventliche Entdeckungen im Alten Testament* (Freiburg, Basel, and Vienna: Herder, 1996; 2nd expanded edition 1998).

Illustration on p. 19 from G. Schmidt, *Die Armenbibeln des XIV. Jahrhunderts* (Graz and Cologne, 1959). Illustrations pp. 38, 42, 43 from M. Schmid, *Die Darstellung der Geburt Christi in der bildenden Kunst* (Stuttgart, 1890).

1   2   3   4   5   6   7   8

Library of Congress Cataloging-in-Publication Data

Dohmen, Christoph, 1957–
    [Von Weihnachten keine Spur? English]
    No trace of Christmas? : discovering Advent in the Old Testament / Christoph Dohmen ; translated by Linda M. Maloney.
        p. cm.
    Includes bibliographical references.
    ISBN 0-8146-2715-3 (alk. paper)
    1. Bible. N.T.—Relation to the Old Testament. I. Title.

BS2387 D595 2000
220.6—dc21   00-027210

Contents

Foreword

For the most part Christians regard the Old Testament as pre-history, a preparation for, or at least a promise of the New Testament and its proclamation of Christ. This is especially true during Advent, when the Christian liturgy intensively, frequently, and in varied ways directs our attention to the promise and its fulfillment. It was therefore a rather daring enterprise for me, in 1996, to present some ideas about Christmas that moved in precisely the opposite direction, namely toward the Old Testament. I was searching for the things in the Old Testament, Israel's Bible, that are necessary and vital for Christians to know if they are to understand the message of Christmas. The response was surprising, and a flood of reactions in conversations, letters, and reviews of the book confirmed for me that there were many people who were glad to join in that quest. This large and intense interest encouraged me to revise the book for a new edition. What has been added to the first edition is owed ultimately to the many readers and audiences whose questions and suggestions brought me farther in my own thinking. As representative of many I want to mention with thanks a few who, one may say, stand behind what is here presented: first of all Paul Deselaers of Münster, whose "biblical spirituality" accompanied the idea of this book from beginning to end—something that will not have gone unnoticed by readers who know him or his work. I also thank Nikolaus Loeb-Ullmann of Berlin, who willingly made available to me a rich fund of material on the Feast of the Circumcision of Jesus, and Hans-Hermann Henrix of Aachen, who during a pre-Christmas workshop pointed out some interesting conclusions to be drawn from what I had presented. I received references to the rich treasury of monastic prayer and meditation from the Benedictine sisters of the Abbey of Herstelle and the Benedictine monks of the Abbey of the Dormition on Mount Zion in Jerusalem. Last but not least I must mention Hubert Frankemölle of Paderborn, whose commentary on Matthew's gospel, now complete, "spurred" and stimulated me in unique fashion.

Apart from a few insertions and additions, this process has led to the writing of three new, brief chapters: "A Gift from Heaven," "In Order That Might Be Fulfilled . . . ," and "Following the Traces."

My continuing thanks go as well to Dr. Peter Suchla of Herder, and to my assistants in Osnabrück, Erika Henze and Ricarda Hovermann, who all helped this work along its way in the most trustworthy fashion.

Osnabrück, 25 March,
nine months before the feast of Christmas 1998

Christoph Dohmen

In Search of Traces

An Introduction

Advent means coming. But who or what is coming? And when or where? The answer seems so simple: Christ comes, of course, at Christmas. But is Advent the same as Christmas? In the Church's liturgy the period surrounding the four Sundays before Christmas is called Advent and is followed by, but clearly distinct from, the Christmas season that begins with the feast. In secular life these distinctions have gradually disappeared. We not only speak of Advent and Christmas together, as if they were the same, but in many places Christmas trees appear in front yards at the beginning of December, and in stores even before Halloween.

The early Church first associated Advent with the idea of Christ's return, after his birth, death, resurrection, and ascension. Advent was a time dedicated to the affirmation in the Christian creed that says ". . . he will come to judge the living and the dead." Accordingly, Advent, understood in that way, marked the end of the Church's year. The new Church year then began with the commemoration of Christ's first coming, his birth. The association in thought and time of the expected return of Christ and the commemoration of his birth in the liturgical year brought it about that the Advent period became a time of preparation for Christmas, and thus came to be the beginning of the Church year.

Its status as end or beginning of the church year shows that Advent is a turning point. It is characteristic of such turning points that one looks back in order to see more clearly where one is and how to move forward into the future. Thus Advent has always been that time in the Church year when Old Testament texts, especially those drawn from Israel's prophecy, were read intensively with a special view to the future. Hence Advent is also the time when Christians are most clearly reminded by the liturgy that they have *one* Sacred Scripture in *two* parts, *one* Bible composed of the Old and New Testaments.

This two-part unity in one book with the special feature that the first and larger part was before and still continues to be the Sacred Scripture of another religion, Judaism, has always posed for Christianity the difficult question of its understanding of its own Sacred Scripture. All too often the apparently easier solution has been sought, namely to act as if the Old Testament did not exist. People saw the decisive and important thing, the "Christian" element, expressed in the New Testament, in contrast to which the First Testament was often regarded as archaic, outdated, and unimportant. To ask Christians why we need the Old Testament at all is often to receive as answer precisely what the selection of liturgical texts for Advent seems to say: these are texts that announce the Messiah and give prophetic notice of his coming.

But the Old Testament contains a great deal more, so that we Christians have to ask ourselves why we do not have an Advent Bible or Christmas Bible, that is, a set of biblical selections that collects all Israel's messianic hopes and promises; instead we have a complete Bible containing the whole Old Testament. What was the reason why early Christianity retained the whole of Israel's Bible as Sacred Scripture, and how did they interpret it?

This little book poses that fundamental question about the basic document of our faith. It is meant to be a little voyage of discovery in thirteen chapters, each of which can be read independently, to take the readers into the Old Testament in search of clues.

In Advent and at Christmas, however, the texts of the liturgy as well as Christian tradition and devotion contain clear traces of the Old Testament. To understand their full meaning, and to discover the faith-convictions that have left those clues and where they lead, it will be necessary to follow the trail of the Christmas spirit back to its source. The chapters in this book begin with a wide variety of images, ideas, and texts from the Advent and

Christmas seasons and, starting from there, follow the traces, often very faint and almost obliterated, into the Old Testament. Thus we will make some *Adventish* discoveries.

Advent means *arriving*. But where do we arrive when we follow these clues? We arrive at the place we came from, at the source of our Christianity, which lies long before Christmas! We may also discover along the way not only the wealth of the Old Testament, but also that that source simultaneously has a great deal to do with our goal as Christians, with the "second Advent" mentioned above. Our own identity, located as it is between Christ's birth and his return, is something we can only discover out of the whole fundamental story of our faith.

Those who accept this book's invitation to a journey of discovery into the Old Testament will encounter a striking contrast: on the one side texts from the New Testament that are so well known that their specific statements and details are all too easily overlooked, and on the other side unknown Old Testament texts that are quite strange and unknown and may even seem rather peculiar at first glance. In order to facilitate access for the readers of this book to both testaments I have made a new translation of all the biblical texts found here, in a very literal and thus often an awkward and aesthetically rather off-putting form. In this way I want to produce a new awareness of the all-too-familiar passages in Scripture, and avoid some misunderstandings of the less-well-known or unknown passages by a closer adherence to the original text. In addition, it would be a happy side effect—and one deliberately aimed at—if these translations were to lead the readers back to the Bible itself because they provoke them to reexamine what is there, or where—that is, in what larger context this or that occurs. That can be discovered by comparing this translation with another.[1] If from the reading of this book come Bible readers who pursue the traces I have pointed out still farther in order to discover still more, the author's idea and purpose in writing this little volume will have been fulfilled.

[1] Translator's note: In most cases the translations for the English edition, where the text does deviate essentially from the author's, have been taken from the New Revised Standard Version.

Finally, I should also point out that in the Old Testament texts the name of God (Yʜᴡʜ), the pronunciation of which has not been handed down to us because the Hebrew text has only its consonants, is always reproduced as Lᴏʀᴅ. This follows Jewish and Christian practice dating from the early translation of the Bible into Greek, when Yʜᴡʜ was rendered as *Kyrios.* Greek *kyrios* is the word for an owner or lord, the one who has the power of decision over another person or a thing. The gender-specific association of "Lord" in English, connected to the pairing of "Lord" and "Lady," is not intended. For a consistent connecting of Old and New Testament texts such a translation is necessary if we are to hear associative connections that the Greek text, for example, creates by its use of the word *kyrios* for the divine name in Old Testament texts.

The title *No Trace of Christmas?* is deliberately given in the form of a question. Perhaps there is, after all, a trace of Christmas in the very places in the Old Testament where we least expect it. And then we may indeed arrive at some "Adventish" discoveries because we will arrive not only in the Old Testament, but with and in ourselves and at a new Christmas—a Christmas that appears to us more clearly and distinctly in a new light, that of the Old Testament.

It All Began Before Christmas

I t is clear enough on the first page of the New Testament that it is not an independent book, even though "book" is its first word. Some translations of Matt 1:1 begin: "The genealogy of Jesus Christ," but the literal beginning is: "The book of the genealogy of Jesus Christ, the son of David, the son of Abraham." This first sentence is not part of the genealogy; if it were, we should properly translate the Greek word *biblos* as "family tree" or "genealogy" or something similar. But the fact that it is not is evident from the two *titles*, "son of David, son of Abraham," that are added after "Jesus Christ." They do not fit the sequence of generations in the genealogy beginning with Abraham that starts in v. 2. Verse 1 is probably to be regarded as the title verse of the whole Gospel of Matthew, which, as was customary in ancient literature, was not clearly set apart from the rest of the text in the way we are used to. If Matthew entitles his work "The Book of the Story of Jesus Christ," he is not yet using the notion of a "book" in the sense we give it, namely a written work bound between two covers and clearly distinct from any other.

Israel and the Nations

Instead, Matthew uses this title to put up a directional sign for readers familiar with Scripture. When they read that formulation they would immediately think of the beginning of the story of humanity in Gen 5:1, described in its title verse as a "book" (NRSV: "This is the list of the descendants of Adam"), but not a "book" in the modern technical sense. Matthew in all probability chose to make this connection to the beginning of human history deliberately, because his gospel describes God's loving care for all humanity and all peoples in the story of this Jesus Christ.

The evangelist underscores the perspective of his gospel again through the two *titles* he inserts: Abraham was later to be seen as the ancestor not only of Israel, but of many nations, and King David became the symbol of Israel's election. Thus in the title of his gospel Matthew allows us to glimpse already that he will be addressing the question of the meaning of this Jesus for the participation of all peoples in Israel's election and its covenant relationship with its God.

The History That Lies Before Us

Once we have grasped the implications of this title sentence that begins Matthew's gospel the genealogy that follows appears in a new light. It, too, helps us see, at the very beginning of this gospel—and thus of the whole New Testament—that this is not an *independent* book. One may expect of an independent, separate book, as of any story, that it will begin by presenting the actors in the story. But Matthew's gospel, with this genealogy, begins in exactly the opposite manner: in the truest sense of the word it presents a chain of forty-four names, forty men and four women, in terms of whom we, as readers, are to locate and understand the principal figure in the story to come, this Jesus Christ. The chain that begins with Abraham undoubtedly represents a progress through Israel's history, which the evangelist presents as the prelude to his story of Jesus. That is: this is no *new* story that begins here, and certainly no *new* book; here is the continuation of something, here something that began long before is going forward, or, to put it the other way around, what is beginning here is not without a prehistory. It can only be understood under the literal precondition of Israel's history, as known to us from Israel's Bible, later called the "Old Testament." Matthew interprets his Jesus-story in terms of this preexisting history of Israel, and he presents his story in light of the theology of Exodus. He does this through an almost concealed reference that only a reader knowledgeable about the Bible will detect. At the conclusion of the genealogy Matt 1:17

summarizes by saying that there were three sets of fourteen generations from Abraham to David, from David to the Babylonian
exile, and from the exile to Christ. If we try to calculate those three
sets of fourteen generations from the names listed we get into difficulties, and this circumstance makes it clear that Matthew is not
giving a mathematical sum here at the end, but pointing to something else. Neither the number fourteen nor the total number,
forty-two, is especially significant in Israel's Bible, and yet the
number contains a hint that was discovered by no less a person
than the famous Church teacher Origen in the third century—
though he was not interested in interpreting Matthew's information. Origen, in fact, discovered this number of forty-two in a
highly interesting summary in Numbers 33, where the stations in
Israel's wandering in the desert are listed in order. If one works
through the long list of places mentioned by Num 33:5-49 between
Egypt and the promised land, there are exactly forty-two. Is
Matthew not nudging the readers of his gospel here to interpret the
history of Israel contained in his genealogy in terms of the Exodus—and that means particularly in terms of the liberating God—
and indeed with this perspective: that with the birth of Jesus the
"land of promise" in a transferred sense has been reached at last? It
is at least worthwhile to read what follows in the gospel once in
that context. The story of the flight into Egypt that follows not long
after (Matt 2:13-17) certainly focuses on interpreting the story of
Jesus in terms of Israel's exodus experience, as the closing quotation from Hos 11:1, "out of Egypt I called my son" underscores. But
if Matthew has focused the view of his gospel so deeply into the
Old Testament with this tiny closing note to his genealogy, we
ought to look more closely at the genealogy itself.

Beginning or End

What kind of genealogy or family tree is this that Matthew
offers us here? Is it the line of Abraham's family, or is it the line of
Jesus' descent?

Genealogies can always be followed in two directions. One
can enter the many branches of followers of a great personality in

a family tree, with that person as the starting point. Or one can collate the numerous ancestors of a person in a genealogical chart in order to show all those who have, in a transferred sense, "entered into" this person. If the first method shows the multitude of descendants, the second points to the multitude of ancestors. The so-called family tree of Jesus at the beginning of Matthew's gospel does neither in a pure form; in a sense it combines both these genealogical methods. It begins with a single person and ends with a single person. In between there is a single linear chain of descendants/ancestors. This procedure, beginning with a single person and ending with a single person, results in the isolation of one line out of the fullness and breadth of the genealogy as a whole.

What is the purpose of such a family tree? Does Matthew simply want to demonstrate that Jesus is a real descendant of Abraham? Or is he honoring Abraham by showing that this Jesus is his greatest descendant? The evangelist clearly rejects both possibilities and makes it quickly obvious to us, his readers, that he is not interested in biological descent, a genealogy in the human sense, because this family tree ends with Joseph who, according to Matthew, is not the father of Jesus, but "the husband of Mary, of whom Jesus was born, who is called the Messiah" (Matt 1:16). The account of the virgin birth that follows in Matt 1:18-25 leaves us in no doubt that the preceding genealogy is of no interest at all as far as the biological descent of this Jesus is concerned. It is therefore not Jesus' biological family tree, but a spiritual family tree for us Christians as readers of the gospel. We are to know from the beginning where our roots and origins as Christians lie, and not whence this Jesus comes.

Remembering Names

Admittedly, we moderns have difficulty with this style. It is not only that genealogies, family trees, and proofs of descent have left a very bad taste in the mouths of Germans since the days of the Nazis in the so-called Third Reich; it is simply difficult for us to discover any story in the simple listing of names. In cases such as the genealogy in Matthew it is not only our lack of biblical knowledge that hinders us from immediately associating the story of this or that person with his or her name; the narrative method itself is strange to us. We like to attach historical traditions to dates. We have learned not only to arrange the great epochs of world history in centuries before and after Christ, but to understand history as a framework of individual dates: the coronation of Charlemagne in Rome, the Crusades, Christopher Columbus's discovery of America, Luther's theses, the Peace of Westphalia, the French Revolution, the Congress of Vienna, the First World War, and so on. Historical traditions that were handed down independently of numbered years are quite different. Here the genealogical framework between the generations fixes the point of departure. The sequence of time, the course of history, is understood in terms of succeeding generations: A begot B, who was followed by C, and so on. Additional traditions and stories can be inserted at the corresponding places in the framework, so that after a while there are major narrative complexes that appear to be interrupted only by minor genealogical passages. Later such an expanded and extensive tradition can again be reduced to key genealogical dates and concentrated so that all the many stories that surround a single person or for which that person has been selected as the nodal point can be briefly and concisely associated with that person.

The evangelist Matthew is doing nothing different when he presents us with the story of Abraham to Joseph/Jesus as a genealogical sequence of names. He has not only the genealogical material available to him, to which he can refer, but also biblical models that he will deliberately recall to his readers' minds through this genealogical prehistory.

Biblically knowledgeable readers of Matthew's gospel will undoubtedly be reminded immediately, when they see this *prehistory* in the form of a genealogical framework, of the books of Chronicles in the Old Testament. The historical summary at the beginning of Chronicles is a kind of summary and conclusion to the Hebrew Bible, in which Chronicles stand at the end of all the books and are not located, as in the Christian Bible, between the other historical books. This tradition in Chronicles begins with a genealogy extending over many pages. To understand what

Matthew is alluding to with his genealogical opening one would really have to read the first ten chapters of 1 Chronicles and immerse oneself in their unique character. A short example drawn from these chains of names may open access to these lists, which admittedly is not an easy matter:

> These are the sons of Israel: Reuben, Simeon, Levi, Judah, Issachar, Zebulun, Dan, Joseph, Benjamin, Naphtali, Gad, and Asher. The sons of Judah: Er, Onan, and Shelah; these three the Canaanite woman Bath-shua bore to him. Now Er, Judah's firstborn, was wicked in the sight of the LORD, and he put him to death. His daughter-in-law Tamar also bore him Perez and Zerah. Judah had five sons in all. The sons of Perez: Hezron and Hamul. The sons of Zerah: Zimri, Ethan, Heman, Calcol, and Dara, five in all. The sons of Carmi: Achar, the troubler of Israel, who transgressed in the matter of the devoted thing; and Ethan's son was Azariah. (1 Chr 2:1-8)

This passage from the great genealogy in 1 Chronicles has a unique feature at the very beginning. The tribe of Judah is selected and placed at the beginning, although it is only fourth in sequence (1 Chr 2:1). If the reader asks what exactly is contained in these few verses he or she quickly sees that different narrative complexes from the so-called patriarchal traditions of the book of Genesis have been brought together here. A clear accent is set by the interruption in the sequence of Judah's sons. After the reference to the death of Er we read immediately of the sons Perez and Zerah, born of Judah's daughter-in-law Tamar, before, or rather in place of Onan and Shelah—something no one could understand unless she or he already knows the story of Tamar in Genesis 38. Here, as in the entire *genealogical prehistory,* knowledgeable readers of the Bible are presupposed, people who not only know all the stories that are merely alluded to here, but who are particularly attentive in discerning the meaning and purpose of the specific genealogical structures, choices, and arrangements.

Who Are We?

If we really undertake such discernment the lists of name after name reveal themselves as a richly theological program. The traditions in Chronicles represent a narrative curve reaching from the beginnings of human history to the new beginning of the people of Israel after the Babylonian exile. The genealogical "anteroom" of Chronicles, as people like to call those chapters, not only presents a time-lapse photo of great epochs in history, but focuses history theologically toward the interesting point by centering all its information on a theology of election. Israel is represented here as the center of the nations, and among the tribes of Israel, in turn, David and his dynasty are shown as the center; finally, the tribes and their territories are characterized in such a way that Jerusalem appears, in this perspective, as the center of Israel, and in the middle of Jerusalem is the Temple, the ultimate dwelling place of God, with its cultic personnel who are listed in detail. This is all about Israel's self-discovery, self-understanding, indeed its very identity. Who and what Israel is as the people of God, as a chosen people, and how someone born into that people should understand himself or herself—those are the questions to which the long genealogical lists in Chronicles offer an answer.

This self-discovery of Israel as the people of God, so important for the new beginning of the nation after the exile, is the foundation for the whole conception of Matthew's gospel and, because that gospel is placed first in the New Testament, for the understanding of the New Testament as a whole. The story of Jesus Christ, and thus the story of Christianity, does not begin with Christmas, but is part of the story of Israel's election and therefore begins, literarily speaking—or perhaps we should say in terms of the techniques of book construction—with Israel's Bible, the later Old Testament. The literary form of genealogy that Matthew chooses in order to show his readers where their own origins, their identity, can be discovered also makes clear that Matthew expects to have readers who are familiar with the Bible. The genealogy acts on us readers almost as a kind of "test" in Scripture, as if it wanted to warn us: remember all this, because you have to know it if you are going to understand the rest of this story of Jesus Christ that I am about to tell you.

The Roots of the Unexpected

Matthew makes clear one particular aspect that he wants to emphasize by not only structuring his genealogical prehistory in three equal parts of 3x14 generations (Matt 1:17), but by including four women within the sequence of forty men. Tamar, Rahab, Ruth, and Bathsheba (the last of whom he simply calls "the wife of Uriah") indicate his purpose. The names of these women are like exclamation points set within the genealogical sequence to make it clear to us readers that this is not merely a list of names, but that there are stories behind them, stories that are filled with life. Here is Tamar, Judah's daughter-in-law, to whom Judah refused to give his third son and who, through a little trick, by dressing as a prostitute, made herself the spouse of her father-in-law and so sidled into the genealogy. Here is Rahab, the prostitute from Jericho, who sheltered Israel's spies and was rewarded by being spared, together with her family, when the city was captured, and being made a part of the people of Israel (Joshua 2; 6). Here is Ruth, the woman of Moab, who refused to abandon her widowed mother-in-law, Naomi, now bereft of the hope of grandchildren, but returned with her to Bethlehem and then secured the continuance of her family (Ruth 4). Finally, here is Bathsheba, the wife of Uriah, whom King David desired and finally married after getting rid of her husband Uriah, and who then became the mother of King Solomon (2 Samuel 11–12). Even when so briefly summarized, the stories of these women are all somewhat unconventional, perhaps even blemishes on an honorable genealogy because they appear to contain so little that is pious or in the nature of a model.

What point does Matthew want to make by including these women? Are all of them, as sinners, meant as a contrast to Jesus' mother Mary so that she will appear in a more glorious light? Or are they meant to show that often it was foreigners, non-Israelites, who by their courage, faith, and strength ensured the survival of the people of God? In this sense Heb 11:31, for example, praises the faith of Rahab, and Jas 2:25 speaks of her courageous action.

Or can it be that Matthew wants to indicate, within this short summary of the history of Israel, that God's ways, God's plan of salvation, ultimately remain opaque to us human beings? We must surely see that God often makes use of things that seem to us odd, and even sinful. The women in that Matthean prehistory disrupt the direct linear genealogy of the men. God's story is not always written in the way people normally expect, by the men who so often set the tone and create the substance of "history." A family tree also represents order and clarity. The tree may branch frequently and grow very tall, but the same lines continue from the roots to the last twigs that keep the tree alive. God's history seems to contradict this image of the tree with all its human calculability. Again and again something new keeps beginning, something that is of course connected with what went before, but not in the way we had humanly expected and planned. When we look at God's story with human eyes it seems that continuity and discontinuity are mutually transformed. There is also the tree that is cut down, that bears no more fruit, but from whose stump, thought to be dead, a new shoot sprouts and brings forth a new growth, because God is faithful. This image from Isaiah 11, well known to us from a Christmas carol ("O, How a Rose E'er Blooming") focuses everything that Matthew's genealogy tries to illustrate through the four women. Will not the one and only God, in the divine fidelity that shows itself also and precisely in the unexpected fulfillment of what has gone before and what has been promised, also be recognized in the virgin birth Matthew will describe, something that is outside every kind of genealogical security? The women in the first New Testament genealogy, and in the stories to which it alludes, sharpen our vision of that truth.

And yet: Jesus did not fall from heaven! He, too, was born into a family, a people. As the genealogies in Chronicles set the family and dynasty of David at their center, because of David's election, so Jesus is born into the people of God as a son of David in order that we Christians may never forget where we belong.

It looks as if we have not very often read the Gospel of Matthew, and with it the New Testament, from the very beginning and with full attention. The history of Christianity again and again shows that Christians have forgotten their Jewish origins, and have even betrayed them. Even the liturgy gives evidence of this misunderstanding or lack of appreciation. The genealogy in

Matthew occurs only once in the entire lectionary, in the gospel reading on Christmas Eve, where it is combined with the story that accompanies it in Matthew, the account of the virgin birth (Matt 1:18-25)—and the latter story may be used alone, without the genealogical prehistory, as a "short version" of the gospel reading. Thus it is suggested that the story of the virgin birth can be understood by itself, without the genealogical prehistory, and that in turn reveals our lack of appreciation for this text.

Advent Is a Time for Scripture

Our Church year does not begin with Christmas, either, but with a preparation for it in Advent. The early Church recognized a time of preparation before the beginning, especially for those who were to be baptized. The time immediately before baptism was devoted primarily to the reading of Scripture, and in the ancient Church that meant the reading and learning of Israel's Bible, the later "Old Testament," which at that time was the Church's only Sacred Scripture. The famous pilgrim nun Egeria mentions in her journal that in fourth-century Jerusalem the bishop went through the Scriptures twice during the forty days before baptism with those who were preparing themselves to receive the sacrament. Against this background it is clear that the New Testament can never be understood in Christianity without the Old, something Matthew also maintains by his use of the genealogy. Indeed, that genealogical prehistory in Matthew stands in the fullest sense of the word *before* the Christmas message of the birth of Jesus Christ. Could we not just once learn to read it as an Advent text, as one in fact *must* read such a genealogy? Day by day and piece by piece we can read the stories of these people in the Old Testament and become aware of them, these people who one after another are listed as father and son, and again father and son—and sometimes also as mothers. Surely then a light would dawn on us at Christmas: namely the understanding that the New Testament is to be read in the light of the Old.

Addressed and Claimed

Y ear after year, in the weeks before Christmas, the bookstores offer us new Bibles as special, elegant Christmas gifts. Of course the old, well-known Bible is not new every year, and in most cases the many new editions do not even offer a new translation that would attempt to bring the Bible's message closer to us in our own language. Instead, what distinguishes these Bibles is their handsome bindings and exclusive presentations. There lies the "normal Bible" with a deeply embossed leather binding and gold lettering, giving the impression of a medieval book, alongside these artistic Bibles in which not only are art works with biblical motifs from this or that artist set within the text, but bear covers that themselves are works of art. One would no more want to handle such a book than one would touch the works of art in museums or exhibitions. And then there are the children's Bibles and comic Bibles, the illuminated Bibles, and all the other editions of the Bible that are made to be a feast for the eyes, and finally the so-called "poor people's Bible."

The fact that "poor people's Bible" is an inappropriate name is especially evident when one looks at the handsome prices of the expensive modern facsimile reproductions of these fascinating medieval pictorial compositions. But even as regards the originals and their intent the name is false, if we understand the name given these "Bibles" to mean that they were Bibles for the poor— whether in the material or the spiritual sense. These medieval assemblages of biblical pictorial motifs have often been called "poor people's Bibles" in reference to Gregory the Great because he once said that pictures are the Bible of the uneducated. Certainly Gregory did not have these special editions of the "poor people's Bible" in mind, but rather meant that those who could not read could often recognize the Bible stories they had heard more easily and quickly with the aid of an illustration. That illustrations or pictorial motifs are often easier of access and remain more deeply embedded in our memories than long speeches and many words is something anyone knows who has children or deals with children. The richly illustrated children's Bibles are ultimately an equally eloquent testimony to what in the truest sense of the word is the impressive character of the image, like a good diagram in a complicated textbook. How often does it happen even for adults that in reading this or that story from the Bible they find they are recalling a picture from their own children's Bible?

But whether the pictures in the so-called "poor people's Bible" were meant to be illustrations in the sense that they made it easier to understand and retain the meaning of biblical stories is more than questionable if one even leafs through such a book. What one sees there are picture pages each containing three pictorial motifs set side by side, and framed by four prophetic figures and sections of text. A quick overview soon reveals that these pictorial compositions bring together things that are widely separated in the Bible itself. While in most cases it is easy to recognize very quickly the New Testament scene set in the middle, the pictures on the right and left, taken from the Old Testament, present some difficulties of understanding because they depict a great many details from Old Testament stories that are scarcely acknowledged in Christian liturgy and catechesis. Here, then, it is really not a matter of illustrated Bible stories, that is, a picture Bible; instead, the "poor people's Bible" presents a pictorial program that is not very easy to understand because we have to learn to *read* it. The key to understanding lies in typology.

In Search of the Proto-Type

Typological thinking attempts to relate separate things, persons, or events by seeking out and describing *correspondences* in order to discover an inner unity.

Even in early Christianity typological thought was increasingly important because Christians were attempting to recognize the unity of salvation history before and after Christ. What was the relationship of God's action in and through Jesus Christ to God's history of election and covenant with the people of Israel? That was the all-important question. It was made concrete in the slowly developing Christian Bible made up of Old and New Testaments as the specific question of the relationship of the testaments to one another, or in other words, the question of the unity of the biblical message. Words, events, persons, and institutions in the Old Testament were regarded as *types* corresponding to words, events, persons, and institutions in the New Testament. The resulting juxtaposition of Old and New Testaments then led to a unity of the story of God with humanity, because through typology the Old Testament was seen as a prototype or foreshadowing of what appeared as a perfected image in the New Testament. Thus, for example, Paul had already represented the connection between sin and redemption as a typology in terms of *Adam* and *Christ.*

There was certainly something positive in this way of looking at the two testaments in terms of typological connections, because it attempted to make vivid the unity of the whole Christian Bible from within itself, and it did not do something that occurs all too frequently in Christianity, namely see the Old Testament as superceded, obsolete, and superfluous, and the New Testament alone as valid or authoritative. Of course, the typological relating of Old and New Testament also contained great danger, as shown by the misunderstanding that has repeatedly appeared on the Christian side, namely that the Old Testament is *only* a prototype, without its own value and independence. Such an idea naturally led, of itself, to a devaluation of Judaism because it had as its Sacred Scripture only what, in typological thinking, was a *precursor* of the New Testament message, even though the Jews are to be regarded as those first called in faith.

If we are aware of this difficulty and reject the negative aspects I have mentioned, then a look at the picture pages of the "poor people's Bible" can certainly be a powerful impulse to faith, because these images lead us in a way scarcely to be found anywhere else from the New Testament message to connections, mainly unknown or less well known, to the first and longer part of our Sacred Scripture, the Old Testament. Indeed, anyone who really looks at these pictures and perhaps even sees a little past the typologies will see New Testament stories and ideas in a new light and learn to understand them more deeply.

The Miracle of the Beginning

If, for example, we look at the depiction of Christ's birth in the "poor people's Bible" we will quickly see that it is not so simple to discover the meaning of this set of images. What does the call of Moses from the "burning bush," sketched on one side, have to do with the birth of Christ? What is the connection between the newborn and the portrayal, on the other side, of the little-known story of the blooming of Aaron's rod? *Reading* this program of imagery presumes that the viewer brings the events depicted to right and left into the picture at the center, so to speak, in order to discover what, in each case, is the corresponding reality.

The first Old Testament example accompanying the picture of the "birth of Christ" has to do with the call of Moses as reported near the beginning of the book of Exodus:

> Moses was keeping the flock of his father-in-law Jethro, the priest of Midian; he led his flock beyond the wilderness, and came to Horeb, the mountain of God. There the angel of the LORD appeared to him in a flame of fire out of a bush; he looked, and the bush was blazing, yet it was not consumed. Then Moses said, "I must turn aside and look at this great sight, and see why the bush is not burned up." When the LORD saw that he had turned aside to see, God called to him out of the bush, "Moses, Moses!" And he said, "Here I am." Then he said, "Come no closer! Remove the sandals from your feet, for the place on which you are standing is holy ground." He said further, "I am the God of your father, the God of Abraham, the God of Isaac, and the God of Jacob." And Moses hid his face, for he was afraid to look at God. (Exod 3:1-6)

The second image has to do with the blooming of Aaron's staff, as reported in the book of Numbers:

> The LORD spoke to Moses, saying: "Speak to the Israelites, and get twelve staffs from them, one for each ancestral house, from all the leaders of their ancestral houses. Write each man's name on his staff, and write Aaron's name on the staff of Levi. For there shall be one staff for the head of each ancestral house. Place them in the tent of meeting before the covenant, where I meet with you. And the staff of the man whom I choose shall sprout; thus I will put a stop to the complaints of the Israelites that they continually make against you." Moses spoke to the Israelites; and all their leaders gave him staffs, one for each leader, according to their ancestral houses, twelve staffs; and the staff of Aaron was among theirs. So Moses placed the staffs before the LORD in the tent of the covenant. When

> Moses went into the tent of the covenant on the next day, the staff of Aaron for the house of Levi had sprouted. It put forth buds, produced blossoms, and bore ripe almonds. Then Moses brought out all the staffs from before the LORD to all the Israelites; and they looked, and each man took his staff. (Num 17:1-9 [MT 17:16-24])

The typological association among these scenes is attested by other witnesses and was therefore known. The miracle that goes against nature is a point of contact among the three images. The thorn bush that is not consumed by fire, the rootless staff of Aaron that puts forth shoots and produces flowers and fruit, both are prototypes for the unimaginable miracle of the virgin birth. But can we be satisfied with such a superficial connection between the images? Is the whole purpose of the entire image composition simply to describe the virgin birth by this means as something beyond nature and therefore a miracle?

The story of Moses does not stop with the miracle. According to the story, Moses' faith is not directed to the miracle of the thorn bush; the latter simply leads him to what is essential, the real matter. The bush that is not consumed attracts Moses' attention, causing him to turn aside to take a closer look. Because of the bush Moses leaves his path, breaks out of his everyday routine. The miracle of the thorn bush brings him to that point, but it is not the purpose of this encounter story. At the moment when Moses allows himself to be drawn by the thorn bush he enters a different world, a world that is new to him. He is addressed and must take off his shoes, the shoes with which he has previously gone his way through life, because the place where he is now standing is "holy ground." This land, a step off the path, is holy only because it is the ground of encounter with God. The miracle of the burning bush has already been forgotten, as far as the story is concerned, and God, who addresses Moses and is thus made known to him, is now the center. But even that is not enough: the story is not interested in telling us that Moses had an encounter with God. Instead, God tells Moses that God has beheld the suffering and oppression of the Israelites and will no longer simply look on; God will deliver Israel out of the hand of the Egyptians and lead them into a land of their own.

A God You Can Talk To

Moses learns the will of God, and he is supposed to translate it into action, to carry out what God wants to do. "I have come down to deliver them from the Egyptians" (Exod 3:8) becomes "come, I will send you . . . to bring my people, the Israelites, out of Egypt" (3:10). Moses may well suspect what kind of burden is being laid on him by this divine command. He cannot take his encounter in the thorn bush with him; he will stand before Pharaoh and before the Israelites as a simple man. But God does not leave him alone; God gives him something to take with him. God reveals the divine name to Moses, and that name is a program. It is not that God thereby says something about the divine essence and nature, as with titles such as "the Strong One," "the Almighty," and so on; no, this name is simply "I am I" (Exod 3:14). Moses can give the Israelites God's own name. Because it is something entirely individual it means more than all the high-sounding or richly expressive names of gods or human beings. Even though the name itself says nothing, it can be used to address God because it is God's name. It is similar to a telephone number that someone might give me. The combination of numbers tells me nothing about that person, but with it I can call, put myself in contact with that person, enter into conversation.

More Than a Miracle

Do we see somewhat deeper when we turn from regarding the burning bush to look at the child in the manger? Is the birth of Christ able to draw us out of our daily round, the worn-out paths of our lives? Does this newborn question our calling? Who addresses us when we approach the manger?

Just as the burning bush is by no means the goal of the story of Moses' call, the second story does not culminate in the fruits of Aaron's blooming rod. Because it draws our attention, it becomes a visible sign. The story maintains this when it follows the section given above, which ends with all retrieving their staffs, by mentioning particularly that only Aaron's blooming rod was to be returned by Moses to the Tent of Meeting to serve as a *sign*. But the staff thus preserved is certainly not only a sign confirming Aaron's election; it is a memorial sign for what happened there. The beginning of the whole episode was the rebellion of the Israelites who joined with Korah and exalted the holiness of the whole people over the special calling of Moses. They refused any longer to recognize Moses' special position and office of leadership (cf. Num 16:3), because they saw no end to the wilderness wandering and felt that in making the Exodus from Egypt they had been betrayed by Moses. Then God stands personally behind Moses and threatens punishment. Only the plea of Moses and Aaron finally causes God's destroying punishment to fall not on the whole people, but only on those who rebelled. These events are then followed by the choice of Aaron to serve as priest at the Tent of Meeting through the miracle of the staffs.

The Demanding Nearness of God

However, this election is not a privilege to be enjoyed by Aaron and his family. Instead they are given special responsibility. The example of those who joined Korah had clearly illustrated for all the Israelites that God's special presence among the people demanded something special from them. The nearness of the God who travels with God's people is not only protection and blessing, but demand. "Normal" life, life like that of everyone else, with the special nearness of God as a bonbon: there is no such thing. Israel learned that again and again, and this often painful lesson is involved in many a biblical story. Aaron's priesthood also represents the special character of Israel's election. Service at the Tent of Meeting mediates that saving nearness of God as well as God's demanding calling of Israel to be God's people. Aaron's rod, blooming and bearing fruit, is the most beautiful and obvious sign of Israel's election, for Aaron's election to serve at the sanctuary can only be understood—in fact, becomes necessary—because of God's immediate presence with this people. However, the fact that the sign of election had to be given at all reminds all those who come after of God's mercy, which makes reconciliation and forgiveness possible, and especially when the special calling and election become a heavy burden.

The pictorial composition in the poor people's Bible, which sets this depiction of Aaron's election through the sign of the blooming staff alongside the picture of the birth of Christ, surely thought also of the background we have just described for this narrative from the book of Numbers, because there is one single passage in the New Testament that mentions this rod of Aaron. It is in the letter to the Hebrews, which in its depiction of the covenant mediated by Christ discusses Israel's sanctuary and mentions the rod of Aaron in the Holy of Holies alongside the altar of incense and the ark of the covenant. The letter to the Hebrews distinguishes the role of Christ in God's plan of salvation very decisively from the Old Testament priesthood. For this author Christ, the mediator, is the High Priest. The ideas connected with that, the associations with the sin offering and redemption, must certainly have suggested the choice of the strange story of the beginning of Aaron's priesthood. The pictorial program in the poor people's Bible means to remind us that with the child in the manger we already have before us Christ, the High Priest, through whom we experience the special closeness of God. It also confronts us with our own election and our special responsibility growing out of it, that in and through Jesus Christ we are to receive a share in Israel's election.

Called and Chosen

How thoughtlessly and apparently lightly we approach the manger, without thinking of who it is that we meet there, without thinking of the consequences of thus approaching! Aaron's blooming staff is a memorial sign. Next to the manger, it should keep us from forgetting that it is God who is here before us. Aaron's service was a ministry at the Tent of Meeting, the place of God's immediate presence. If God has become human in this Jesus, we could say that we slip into the role of Aaron and enter into the Holy of Holies, the place of God's immediate presence.

If we sense a little of the depth of the ideas in this pictorial scheme in the poor people's Bible we sense how the composition calls us into question because in light of the manger it demands that we give an account of our faith. If we encounter God in Christ, if we Christians overcome all barriers between God and humanity—here at the manger in Bethlehem—then this is no more a privilege than was Aaron's service at the Tent of Meeting. The privilege consists, at most, in a special responsibility: to give testimony to the presence of God.

Do other people sense or experience that we Christians are celebrating the earliest beginning of our closeness to God at Christmas? All too often even we probably do not get to the heart of the Christmas message. We get stuck somewhere in the hectic preparation for Christmas and probably can no longer find our way to the child in the manger. It seems as if our life is deficient in spectacle and fascinating theatre, so that we cannot stand still, like Moses, and turn our whole attention to an unexplainable detail by the side of the road.

However, the small step is necessary, and so is the will to see and understand. Can we afford to stand still in order to turn to the thing that is on the margin? Time goes on, and Christmas gets closer and closer. . . . But whether at Christmas God can really come a little closer to us, encounter and address us—it all depends on our readiness to stop, to pause, and to look for meaning.

The artists who made the poor people's Bible tried to understand. They place before our eyes what the birth of Christ means for our own self-understanding by bringing such apparently irrelevant things as the call of Moses at the burning bush and the election of Aaron through the blooming of his staff close to the Christmas event. The clue they thus lay down leads deep within the Old Testament, into its center, for there between Egypt and the promised land, there at the mountain of God, Israel finds its identity and becomes the people of God. At Christmas, so the pictorial composition in the poor people's Bible tries to tell us, nothing completely new begins; instead, God's long history with Israel reaches a new climax. Those who will meet God in this Jesus meet Moses and Aaron as well. For it is only Israel's experience of God's nearness and Israel's response to God's word throughout its long history that give a foundation to the faith that it is God in person who approaches us in this child in the manger. It is only through Moses and Aaron that the size and power of the Christmas message become clear to us. Christmas: the feast of our calling and election. To understand that we must go deep down to the sources of our faith in the Old Testament. There is no New Testament without an Old Testament, and no witness to Christ without the Torah of Moses.

Regarded rightly, the pictures in the poor people's Bible may in fact make us rich—and not only at Christmas.

A Gift from Heaven

I n the days before Christmas many of us look at the sky, or at the weather report, for signs to show us whether there will be snow for Christmas. The idyllic image of a "white Christmas" has marked us deeply, even though the biblical texts and prayers say nothing about snow: rain, more likely. "Shower, O heavens, from above, and let the skies rain down righteousness" is one of the liturgy's antiphons, drawn from Isa 45:8: "let the earth open, that salvation may spring up, and let it cause righteousness to sprout up also." Behind this image is the Near East's life-and-death idea of divine blessing, the gift of rain and dew from heaven. The high symbolic value attributed to dew in biblical texts apparently goes back to the natural experiences of people in the Holy Land; they simply observed what a life-giving effect the often heavy summer dew produced in the time when there was no rain. Who can be surprised if dew became a sign of divine blessing, or that it appears in a story about God's care for Israel's survival? "In . . . the morning there was a layer of dew around the camp" (Exod 16:13) we read in the famous story of the bread from heaven, the manna that God gave the people as food on their route through the wilderness. As dew can give living things the water they need, just so the Israelites receive their bread, quite apart from any human influence, as a gift from heaven.

Gideon's Fleece

Another, somewhat strange-sounding story in the Old Testament plays on this gift of God, using "dew" as a keyword.

Then Gideon said to God, "In order to see whether you will deliver Israel by my hand, as you have said, I am going to lay a fleece of wool on the threshing floor; if there is dew on the fleece alone, and it is dry on all the ground, then I shall know that you will deliver Israel by my hand, as you have said." And it was so. When he rose early next morning and squeezed the fleece, he wrung enough dew from the fleece to fill a bowl with water. Then Gideon said to God, "Do not let your anger burn against me, let me speak one more time; let me, please, make trial with the fleece just once more; let it be dry only on the fleece, and on all the ground let there be dew." And God did so that night. It was dry on the fleece only, and on all the ground there was dew. (Judg 6:36-40)

This is a wondrous story that at first glance has nothing to do with the life-giving power of the dew, but simply links it with a peculiar sign. But the sign is part of the story of Gideon's call. The angel of the Lord had appeared to him and greeted him with: "The LORD is with you" (Judg 6:12), but Gideon's response was marked by depression and despair. It would be nice if God were with me, Gideon's answer conveys, and he asks where he can find God's presence, God's help, where all the wonderful deeds the ancestors told of may be for him and his. He thinks that God has rejected and abandoned God's people. Like Moses at the burning bush, he receives a gigantic assignment: "Deliver Israel!" (Judg 6:14). And like Moses when he was called, Gideon hesitates and points out to God that his tribe is the weakest and he is the youngest in his family. But God promises to be with him, and still the one called hesitates, wanting a sign in order to be entirely sure. . . . The sign is given him in fire that devours his sacrifice. When, at the beginning of the passage quoted above, Gideon again hesitates over his task, the strange sign with the fleece opens up its meaning. The task is too great, and the subject feels himself too weak. Again, just as Moses had required two signs to affirm his mission—the serpent staff and the leprous hand—so Gideon needs another sign to gather courage for his call. And even this second sign shows how hesitant and fearful is this man whom the angel of the Lord had previously addressed as a "mighty warrior." It happens just as Gideon had asked: the ground is dry and the fleece is saturated with dew. The narrative moves forward in rapid strides, but whoever

looks carefully and listens with sharp ears to what is going on behind the words of the story will hear and sense the whispering
doubt of the hero. What has happened could have been entirely
natural. The rapidly rising temperature in the morning could of
course dry up the dew on the flat threshing floor, while the fleece
would hold it longer. Gideon wants, indeed he must have clarity.
The special, the unnatural, the inexplicable must happen here in
order that Gideon may know that God will deliver Israel through
him. But Gideon also senses some unease: he could go too far in
his demands and call down God's wrath on him. Like a pleading
child he repeatedly emphasizes: "Just this one more time." And
God seems to understand that Gideon needs just this, and without
a word lets it be so: the wetness of the dew lies on the whole flat
floor, while the fleece is dry. The story need not tell us that Gideon
believed, and accepted and carried out his task; what follows
shows us that. But the strange sign with the fleece and the dew is
certainly meant not merely to fix our attention on the hesitant
hero, the one called, but also to give an interpretation to his story
as a tiny mosaic piece in the whole history of the people of God.
The dew that God allows to fall from heaven as a sign for Gideon
deliberately recalls the manna, the bread from heaven, that en-
abled Israel to survive in the wilderness. Deliverance and salvation
are in the foreground of the story of Gideon. Twice the little
episode has Gideon remind God that God will "deliver" Israel. Israel's salvation is due not to Gideon's military might and that of
his men; it is not strategy or military superiority that bring deliverance to Israel, but Gideon the judge, who finds his divine calling
as Israel had found the bread from heaven in the wilderness: as
dew on the ground.

More Than a Name

To proclaim the man Jesus, to explain who he is, Christians
very early sought stories in Israel's Bible that expressed this salvation, the deliverance of Israel. Not only the keyword "salvation,
deliverance," which is also contained in the name "Jesus," led their
search to the story of Gideon, but also the angel of the Lord, who

according to Luke 1:28 greeted Mary with the same words as those addressed to Gideon: "The Lord is with you." Having discovered the story of Gideon, then, Christians quickly recognized that the salvation come to the world in Jesus is a gift of heaven like the manna in the wilderness that lay like dew on the ground, and like the dew that confirmed for the hesitant Gideon that he was to deliver God's people.

Deliverance and salvation from Israel's God: that is what Christians experienced in the birth of Jesus as a gift from heaven, and therefore they took the story of Gideon as a sign to be used to explain it. In the Middle Ages the story of Gideon's fleece was placed among the typological images in the so-called "poor people's Bible" opposite the annunciation to Mary, and many liturgical texts in use even today have developed the idea still further. The sign of the dry fleece on the wet ground, setting aside the laws of nature, became in Christian interpretation a reference to Mary's virginity, and Jesus himself, who brought God's deliverance and redemption to humanity, could be represented in the image of the dew as God's gift, the gift of heaven.

Perhaps we may hesitate and doubt like Gideon when we sing "Drop down dew, you heavens, from above, and let the clouds rain the Just One" during Advent, and we cannot imagine that God wants to address us in Jesus' birth in order, through Jesus, to take us with him into the salvation of God's people Israel. In the programmatic name "Jesus," Gideon's task, to "deliver Israel," is positively laid at our feet, at Christmas, but not only then, as a gift from heaven, like dew on the ground.

When Shepherds Become Prophets

I f you look at some of our Christmas crib scenes you would get the idea that whole tribes spent the night outdoors with the flocks in the fields around Bethlehem, for here we see adults and children, old men and mothers with nursing infants, all hurrying to the stable. Luke's gospel, however, says only that there were shepherds keeping watch in the fields. Certainly it would have been only a few individuals, not whole families. Nomadic families who lived in tents were no longer found in the neighborhood of Bethlehem in Jesus' time, and they were in any case surely not what the evangelist Luke had in mind when he spoke of the shepherds watching over their flocks by night.

But why does the angel appear to these shepherds? Were they simply those closest, in the truest sense of the word? Is the idea that the first people had better get to the manger as quickly as possible, to adore there? Or do these shepherds just fit best with the place of the birth, the stable and the manger?

In Luke's gospel the angel's message to the shepherd is: "I am bringing you good news of great joy for all the people" (Luke 2:10). The meaning and purpose of the news that comes to the shepherds is great joy for Israel, for the whole people. The reason for that joy is described by the angel: "to you is born this day in the city of David a Savior, who is the Messiah, the Lord" (Luke 2:11). But then the angel speaks, oddly enough, of a sign. The angel does not say "you will find him, the Messiah, here, or there, or this way." No, the message is that they, the shepherds, will find a child wrapped in bands of cloth and lying in a manger: that is the sign for them. A sign always points to something else, something it is not. But what will a child in a manger point to?

Signs play a great part in the lives of Israel's prophets. Usually they are to serve as a confirmation for those who are addressed by God through the prophets, evidence that a true prophet, sent and commissioned by God, is speaking to them, so that his or her message really comes from God and is God's word. There is no reason to think that the shepherds mistrusted the angel and therefore need that kind of sign as confirmation. But the angel did not proclaim "great joy" for the shepherds; the message was "great joy" for all Israel. There is surely a prophetic task in that. The angel opens heaven to the shepherds, so to speak. They are given a glimpse into a little bit of God's saving plan for humanity. But since it is for the whole people, they receive a sign that will confirm for others that they, the shepherds, are really speaking for God.

Those who see all this and know Israel's Bible, for Christians the Old Testament, will be especially alert. The keywords are all too clear: the region of Bethlehem, the shepherds, God's message, and the prophetic commission.

The Prophet Who Leaves the Flock

Amos was the Old Testament prophet whom God "took from following the flock" (Amos 7:15). In a dispute with the priest Amaziah at the shrine at Bethel, where God had sent him, Amos emphasizes that he is no prophet, but a "herdsman," and this shepherd, who appears at the central sanctuary of the northern kingdom of Israel in the eighth century B.C.E., is more precisely described in the introduction of the book named for him as a shepherd of Tekoa (Amos 1:1). Tekoa is a tiny village in the southern kingdom of Judah, in the region of Bethlehem.

We only have to think of this Amos when we read Luke's gospel and hear of shepherds who were watching by night in that region, and who received a message from God for the whole nation of Israel. In the book of this prophet Amos, whom God took from the flock to make God's messenger, this kind of call and commissioning is described:

> "Do two walk together unless they have made an appointment?
> Does a lion roar in the forest, when it has no prey?

Does a young lion cry out from its den, if it has caught nothing?
Does a bird fall into a snare on the earth, when there is no trap for it?
Does a snare spring up from the ground, when it has taken nothing?
Is a trumpet blown in a city, and the people are not afraid?
Does disaster befall a city, unless the LORD has done it?
Surely the Lord GOD does nothing, without revealing his secret to
    his servants the prophets.
The lion has roared; who will not fear?
The Lord GOD has spoken; who can but prophesy?" (Amos 3:3-8)

The images employed here are strong; they speak for themselves. All of them relate to the immediately apparent relationship between cause and effect. Nothing happens without a reason; one thing brings about another. The text expresses this natural necessity, its obvious character and evident truth, in rhetorical questions. The only answer to the first six questions is "no, that would not happen!" and the seventh, shaped in the same way, demands the same answer. But this seventh question takes us outside the known and obvious realm of nature. Now God enters the picture. The question does not begin with the philosophical idea of the first cause, to which everything described before could be traced back, but with something in concrete experience. The one who ultimately causes disaster for a city determines the fate of the people in it. This is because God is God, and is behind everything, and because nothing can happen without God.

And God Behind Everything?

But the text in Amos has not yet reached its goal with that statement. It goes a step farther. It looks at God's intention, the plan behind everything that happens in our human lives. So, after the seventh question, there comes the first statement. It follows on the action of God in the last question and asserts that God does nothing without first revealing it to the prophets and, through the prophets, letting the people themselves know of it.

Now we are in the realm of the "supernatural," of revelation, and no longer of natural necessity and things that one can learn in and through nature. Not only what God conveys to the prophets is revelation; even the statement that God does nothing without first revealing it through prophets must be understood as revelation. Of course it follows as a matter of course from the self-evidence inherent in rhetorical questions like those that precede it in the text from Amos, and its obvious intent is that one should transfer the self-evidence from one to the other, but that is precisely where the heart of this statement lies. As clear as the examples from human life are, it should be just as clear that God announces everything God is about to do through prophets. One can probably see and understand that only in retrospect, in view of the many prophetic messages, even though we well know that they often remain unheard.

This idea about prophetic proclamation takes us one step further. It is directed not only to those who should realize that God does nothing without prophetic prediction, and who therefore ought to listen to the voices of the prophets, but also and especially to the prophets themselves. What God does, God reveals beforehand to the prophets. That also means that "prophet" is not a freely-chosen profession; the one who hears God's word and has God's decision revealed to her or him must become a prophet.

How Do You Become a Prophet?

Our ordinary language has reduced "prophet" to the fundamental meaning of the root word "prophecy": prediction or announcement of something future. In this sense we like to say about anything that we can expect or anticipate that you don't need to be a prophet to know this or that. On the other hand, we say of people who have feared, seen, or communicated something unexpected or unanticipated that they are prophets. This kind of language can be traced to the special characteristics of Christian theology, which for a long time spoke of Israel's prophets, that is, those who are known to us from the Old Testament, almost exclusively in terms of their having predicted the saving events that came about in Jesus Christ. This point of view, which, beginning from that concept of prophecy, has more or less pressed the whole of the Old and New Testaments into the mold of "promise and fulfillment," has left its residue in countless pieces of Christian art. In contrast, if we look at the multiplicity of prophetic phenomena we find in the Old Testament we quickly observe that through these spectacles of "promise and fulfillment" we are seeing only a tiny segment. We even encounter groups of prophets in the Old Testament (ecstatics, students of the prophets, royal or court prophets) as well as individuals (e.g., Gad or Nathan, Samuel or Elijah, the woman prophet Huldah or the so-called writing prophets Isaiah, Jeremiah, and Ezekiel). In its Greek translation the Old Testament calls all these people, for the most part without distinction, "prophets," while in Hebrew there is a spectrum of fine distinctions among "men of God, persons called/appointed, seers," etc. Despite all this variety of prophecy in Israel, the most important element is always that the persons in question understand themselves to have been called (appointed) by God and sent with a message. They do not proclaim what comes from their own spirits or hearts, as, for example, Ezek 13:2 emphasizes is the case with the false prophets; the principle for them is that expressed by the so-called messenger's speech that begins or ends prophetic utterance: "The LORD has spoken," or "word of the LORD."

From this understanding of the calling/appointment of the prophets also comes the necessity for the one called to prophesy, indeed, the compelling pressure to do so. This inward pressure is emphasized in the passage above from the book of Amos by the fact that, after the statement that God does nothing without first telling the prophets, there are two more rhetorical questions dependent on what has gone before. In the end they leave no doubt of the inevitability of the prophets' call. There is no need for a special spiritual education preceding the call, nor is assent needed. When God's word comes, the one it reaches is a prophet. We see that not only in Amos, but also in other Old Testament prophets who at first try to avoid becoming prophets because they sense the burden that comes with it.

The shepherds watching in the fields near Bethlehem during the night are quite simply made prophets by the message the angel brings them. They are taken from their flocks. Arriving in Bethlehem, they find the child in the manger, as predicted. There they tell what was said to them about this child (Luke 2:17). Thus the prophetic task of the shepherds on behalf of the whole of Israel is made manifest, for the evangelist Luke says that all who heard it were amazed at what the shepherds told them (2:18). The evangelist does not say who was present in the stable when the shepherds arrived. He is much more interested in the fact that the message the shepherds were to proclaim reached the people, and he uses the word "amazed" because they did not just hear something, but what they heard moved and touched them at the deepest level.

Mary Understands

Luke uses Mary, who in this gospel has already been made aware of the uniqueness of her child through the proclamation of the angel Gabriel (Luke 1:26-38), to make still clearer, in the response to the words of the shepherds, what *understanding* really means. "Mary treasured all these words and pondered them in her heart." That, or something close to it, is what we read in most English translations. Literally the text says at this point that Mary kept everything together and gathered the words in her heart. This way of describing understanding is something like a puzzle. You gather the pieces, put them in order, and then put them together. Only when every piece is in its place can the meaning of the whole picture be seen. Mary brings what she heard from the shepherds together with what she herself had heard from the angel; she puts the things together, and in this way she understands.

Is not the evangelist giving us here, at the very beginning, a key for understanding the tradition about Jesus? Don't we have to collect quite a lot of things before we can put them all together to form a single picture? In this sense, must we as Christians not become deeply acquainted with Israel's Bible, our Old Testament, in order to bring it together with the proclamation of Jesus Christ, and so to understand, through the whole history of God with humanity, what God wants from us today? Is not Luke, with his reference to Mary's understanding, pointing to an understanding of the later New Testament message, which is not something new or different in contrast to the message of the Old Testament, but proves to be a further set of pieces in God's great puzzle, which we are called to put in the right places?

Seeing Through the Prophets' Spectacles

The shepherds fulfilled their prophetic commission. Like Amos, who for a short time was called away from the flocks in order to prophesy, they too were able to return to their flocks; everything had happened "as it had been told them" (Luke 2:20). This conclusion with which Luke ends the story of the shepherds underscores the prophetic nature of their appearance at the manger, for the fact that what has been announced really happens as foretold is an important point in biblical tradition: it helps to distinguish between true and false prophecy. Thus, for example, in Deuteronomy we read:

> "You may say to yourself, 'How can we recognize a word that the LORD has not spoken?' If a prophet speaks in the name of the LORD but the thing does not take place or prove true, it is a word that the LORD has not spoken. The prophet has spoken it presumptuously; do not be frightened by it." (18:21-22)

With this story about the shepherds who act as prophets Luke proposes something that is quite central to Christianity. He lets us, as readers and hearers of his gospel, know from the beginning that the message of Christ is not something entirely new that has fallen from heaven, but that it has its basis in God's revelation to Israel.

Later prophecy as a whole will even become the key to Christian understanding of the Old Testament. Externally this is evident simply from the fact that in the Christian Bible the prophetic books are placed at the end of the Old Testament, that is, immediately before the New Testament, while in the Jewish Bible they are to be found in the middle, directly after the books of the Torah (Genesis through Deuteronomy). According to Jewish understanding the "prophets" include the books of Joshua, Judges, Samuel, and Kings, because they contain stories about prophets (for example, Samuel, Nathan, Elijah, Elisha) and were written in the prophetic spirit.

The prophetic perspective to be found in Christianity, which at first regarded major parts of Israel's Bible, and later almost the whole of it, as prophecy, is, of course, not a Christian invention. In the time surrounding Jesus' birth there seem to have been a number of Jewish groups who expected, hoped, or feared the end of time, that is, the inbreaking of the reign of God, and therefore read their sacred Scripture, the Bible of Israel, as prophetic prediction of the end.

There are clear examples of this in the writings discovered beginning in 1947 in the caves at Qumran on the Dead Sea. Here there are not only commentaries that apply the known prophetic books verse for verse to the present time of the community living there, but in a great many fragments from Cave 4 we find messianic expectations that are very close to those known to us from the New Testament. Thus in one fragment we even find a formulation like that in Luke 1:32 about the "son of the Most High" (4Q 246). These messianic texts and formulations, however, do not point to an equation with or dependence of the authors of the Qumran documents on Christianity, but more properly to the spiritual and intellectual currents in Judaism of the time. The similarity or absolute likeness of the material, that is, is often a matter of course, because all these groups within Judaism had the same sacred Scripture. The Christians also, for a long time—well into the third century—knew only Israel's Bible as their sacred Scripture, but they read it more from the perspective of the prophets, while the principal currents in Judaism saw its focus in revelation, that is, Torah. When the letter to the Hebrews says at the very beginning that God spoke many times and in many ways to the ancestors through the prophets (Heb 1:1), we have clear evidence of the Christian view of the Old Testament as prophecy, because the multiplicity of revelations thus referred to certainly goes beyond the narrower sphere of the prophetic books.

Thus Luke, with his Christmas story, is entirely within the current of this prophetic view of Israel's Bible; indeed, he even prepares the way for its specific Christian version.

Then are the shepherds Luke writes about the first Christians as far as he is concerned? Do they already confess this Jesus as the

Christ, the Messiah of Israel? He says nothing about that. To begin with, it is clear that the shepherds simply return to their previous lives, like Amos before them. They did not become Christians; they became prophets! Thus they stand within the sequence of Israel's prophets.

The reference to Amos directs our attention to the truth that God does nothing without first informing the prophets (cf. Amos 3:7). And the shepherds as prophets lead to the prophets of Israel. That means that they point the readers and hearers of the gospel to the Old Testament, for in the way of thinking common at that time the whole Old Testament—as we have seen—was frequently regarded as prophecy.

The connection between shepherd and prophet was probably noticed very early. There is scarcely any other explanation for the fact that in the oldest depictions of the birth of Christ we find a shepherd and a prophet as interpretive representatives—for example on part of a sarcophagus lid from the second half of the fourth century, where we find beside the manger, beside the ox and ass, a shepherd, recognizable from his staff, and a prophet with the scroll of Scripture in his hand.

The story of the shepherds at Bethlehem accordingly leaves us in no doubt that Christians *must* read Israel's Bible, their Old Testament, in order to understand the message about Christ, and in the truest sense of the word they must read it from the very beginning.

The Message of Israel's Enduring Election

The shepherds and the message given to them again underscore for us that what is at stake here is Israel's election, not a new religion to be founded by Jesus. The shepherds, who in the context of Luke's history are obviously Jews, must not and should not abandon their Judaism and become Christians, as was all too often demanded of their Jewish fellow citizens by Christians of later times, when they had seized the reins of power. If only they had taken a closer look at the shepherds at the manger!

After all, the angel had clearly told them that this was a great joy for the whole people, that is, for Israel. Luke, who is writing his gospel after Easter, in light of the resurrection, so to speak, knows and of course wants the readers of the good news also to know that they are not just supposed to return to their daily lives, as the shepherds did, but to find their way to faith in this Jesus, the Christ. But the shepherds are at the same time their model, because they followed the message that came to them; they became prophets, if only for a short time. Like Amos, they could not withstand the word of God that struck them. Thus they clarify for us the fact of Israel's enduring election and warn us who confess Jesus as Christ that we should not lose sight of that fact. For our share in Israel's election, as described in Luke's Christmas story, also demands of us an accounting of our faith. This reinforces for us also the words of Amos that turned our attention to Luke's story of the shepherds, because they are introduced by the idea of election and accounting:

> Hear this word that the LORD has spoken against you, O people of Israel, against the whole family that I brought up out of the land of Egypt: "You only have I known of all the families of the earth; therefore I will punish you for all your iniquities." (Amos 3:1-2)

For Amos, as for the shepherds at Bethlehem, it is certain that one must become a prophet when God's word comes. And what will we be, as we look at the shepherds at the manger, in the face of the Word of God made flesh? Will we be new people addressed by that word, or will we just be touched fleetingly by this idyll of shepherds as we plunge into the Christmas rush?

You Shall Make No Crib for Yourself!

Anyone who steps out of the hectic world of modern society and enters a church quickly experiences that space, with its subdued lighting and atmosphere of repose, as a counter-world in contrast to the driving pace of the streets. An artist called upon a few years ago to propose a sketch for such a space took up this idea of a counter-world and considered how he might create an "imageless zone" as protection against the visual flood in our multimedia world. To accomplish this he followed the biblical prohibition: "You shall not make for yourself an idol . . ." (Exod 20:4; Deut 5:8). But since the church, unlike a gallery or a museum, does not stand empty until it is filled with pictures, but instead is the gathering place of a community, the community itself should also contribute its own "mental image." It did so in this case by asking people in public life what the Old Testament commandment, "you shall not make for yourself an idol," meant for them today. One answer was a question: "If I am not allowed to make an image of God, can I still set up a Christmas crib?" (Katharina Schwamborn).

Image of the Invisible God

In the first centuries of Christian history the answer to that question would certainly have been "no." For the early Christians there was no way to picture God, because God is greater than and utterly different from anything people can imagine. Even when they attempted to depict God, what was revered in the picture produced was ultimately something absolutely distant from God, namely the material object, the beauty and value of the image or the artistic talent that had produced it. Thus early Christianity held fast to the fundamental meaning of the so-called second commandment. And when some arose who argued that God had, after all, become human in Jesus, so that while one may not make an image of God it was after all possible to depict the human face of God, become visible in Jesus, in human form, others objected that that would be to suppress Jesus' divinity because only his humanity could be imaged.

Thus the early Christians did not deal lightly with the question of images, and only slowly were images of Jesus allowed because, as a human being, he is, so to speak, the only visible form of God, as is written in the hymn in Col 1:15: "He is the image of the invisible God, the firstborn of all creation." Therefore in subsequent years one finds the image of Christ in Old Testament scenes, since depiction of God remained forbidden in Christian art until the high Middle Ages. Only when people began to pictorialize the various statements of the Christian creed was the image of Christ alone no longer adequate. The relationship between Father and Son was at first so depicted that the same figure appeared as an older and a younger man.

A Human Being in the Manger

Thus we should not be at all surprised that for a long time Christianity did not have a Christmas crib. The custom of making manger scenes with figures and setting them up to be looked at and venerated at Christmas first arose in the Middle Ages. According to one story it was Francis of Assisi who, on Christmas in 1223, led the people of the Italian city of Greccio out of town to a stable where living people and animals portrayed the Christmas gospel, so as to make the uniqueness of God's "incarnation" clear to them. The rich tradition of the Christmas crib and Christmas plays then developed from this idea of illustrating the incarnation.

Of course there had already been depictions of the birth of Christ in art before 1223, because as soon as people began portraying scenes from the life of Jesus the image of the child in the manger and the stable in Bethlehem, as the starting point for Jesus' life story, were quite naturally among the things depicted.

For the depiction of the scene people were and are dependent almost exclusively on Luke's infancy narrative, because the evangelists Mark and John report nothing of Jesus' birth and childhood, and Matthew mentions the fact of the birth only briefly before continuing with the account of the visit of the three Wise Men. Luke tells us something more about why Jesus was born in Bethlehem, and that he entered the world in a stable and was laid in a manger "because there was no place for them in the inn" (Luke 2:7)—and he tells of the shepherds who were told by an angel about "the child in the manger." We search in vain for everything else that we would like to know for the sake of preparing our crib scene.

Were there other people in this emergency shelter, others who found no room in the inn? Were the people sheltered alongside animals, or was the stable empty? Where was this stable: somewhere out in the pastures, or in the village, next to the inn? (Matthew only mentions a house in which the Magi find the child and his mother.) Was it a low-roofed shelter for sheep and goats, or a larger building for big animals?

We learn nothing of that in the New Testament, and for that very reason it is surprising that, long before the shepherds' sheep can be found in these Christmas scenes, not one of them lacks *an ox and a donkey.* We could almost get the impression that someone or other knew something about this ox and donkey that the evangelists no longer remembered, or had overlooked. A search for this apparently lost tradition about the ox and ass at the manger is pretty exciting. We find no story or reference to anyone at all who at any time might have retained a memory of an ox and a donkey; nevertheless, what we do find are the oldest pictorial representations of the Christmas message in Christianity—and they do not show what we would expect, Mary and Joseph and the child in the manger, but only the child in the manger, flanked by—an ox and a donkey!

The infant with ox and ass is a strange ensemble, quite unreal and unnatural. Whoever depicted something like that, while simply omitting Mary and Joseph, who really belong in the center of the picture and, after all, are found in the gospel, so as to reduce the whole picture to ox, donkey, and child cannot have meant to depict some special memory of the circumstances of Jesus' birth. Whoever made that picture must have meant to tell those who looked at the picture something else.

Between Ox and Ass

If we realize that this is not about a representation of the real conditions after the child's birth, and that this is not the first snapshot of the newborn for the family album, the individual elements of the picture will quickly lead us to what the artist wanted to say. The starting point for the composition is the key word "manger," which appears three times in the Lukan infancy gospel (Luke 2:7, 12, 16), and which led the Church Fathers to make a connection with Isa 1:3: "The ox knows its owner, and the donkey its master's crib."

Thus the oldest Christian images of Christmas allude to this interpretation; we might say that by means of the ox and ass and the manger with the child they associate an Old Testament passage with the Christmas message, in order, then, to interpret the

Christmas event on the basis of the whole of Sacred Scripture. Among the Church Fathers' interpretations of this passage from Isaiah we find the interpretation that the ox and ass represent the Church made up of Jews and Gentiles, who recognize their Lord in the manger, while Israel does not recognize him, as alluded to in the following verse from Isaiah. We then find more extensive interpretations reading the ox and ass, as clean and unclean animals, in terms of Israel and the Church, and interpretations that associate the Isaiah passage with the Latin text of Hab 3:2, which reads "between two living creatures you will be made known." This passage from Habakkuk also played a special role in the Good Friday liturgy as an interpretation of the death of Jesus between the two criminals, so that here, with the connection between the ox and ass and the two living creatures, a line is drawn between Jesus' birth and death.

However, as concerns the early Christian images that introduced Isa 1:3 into the Christmas story by means of the ox and ass, we should not be too hasty in restricting their significance to one or another interpretation by the Church Fathers. It is rather a question of a fundamental offer of interpretation, a trace that is laid down to enable us to understand the birth of Christ in terms of the history of salvation. The observer must, of course, not make the Old Testament passages there presented the object of a modern examination of the biblical evidence; instead, one must "weave in" the passage in its context as a background in order to understand what happens in and with the birth of Jesus. In this way the Christmas message can develop its significance for each individual.

The verse cited, with the ox and ass, is at the very beginning of the book of Isaiah. It not only inaugurates the first "woe" and the message of judgment in the first chapter, but the whole prophetic book as well:

> "Hear, O heavens, and listen, O earth;
> > for the LORD has spoken:
> I reared children and brought them up,
> > but they have rebelled against me.
> The ox knows its owner,

and the donkey its master's crib;
but Israel does not know,
my people do not understand." (Isa 1:2-3)

The call to "hear," which is read over quickly as a rhetorical flourish, is revealed as highly significant, for it is addressed to heaven and earth and thus shows that the relationship between Israel and its God that is then addressed has a global significance in the fullest sense of the word. This is not a situation that God will deal with quietly and in secret with God's people; no, what God speaks of here is world-shaking: it has effects and consequences far beyond Israel. God describes the situation briefly and concisely in the image of a parent and children. God really had made something of Israel, had "reared" them and "brought them up" like sons and daughters, as the text literally says. When, then, they are confronted with the way they have broken with God in reaction, the text at first sounds all too human, like the reproach of a disappointed and angry parent whose children have shown themselves ungrateful in the parent's eyes by adopting other ways than those the father and mother have shown them. But that this is *not* the issue here, but only a description of the situation, is clear from the image from the animal world that follows immediately. The image does not refer to the false expectation of a necessary gratitude or a demand for obedience, but to the matter-of-fact way in which animals recognize their owners, those who feed them.

Liberated and Chosen

To know where we belong, what and who keeps us alive, seems like the simplest and most natural thing in the world, something natural even to the beasts, who lack rationality. Therefore it is astonishing that Israel does not know this, and shows by its behavior that it cannot make a distinction (the literal translation of "do not understand") between what it has received and what it does for itself.

The whole passage thus culminates in God's standing amazed before Israel's behavior. Israel's way of life is impossible to understand, because its break with God is the equivalent of cutting itself off from life. Would an ox or ass ever turn away, in any comparable fashion, from the food placed before it?

What God did when God "reared children and brought them up" can be briefly summarized in the liberating action of the Exodus and the election of Israel as God's people, which is why here, at the end of the passage, God emphatically calls Israel "my people." This last leads directly back to the starting point of the speech, namely that what is being addressed here is of concern to the entire world: for the election of Israel, in biblical understanding, is not a privilege that will place Israel in a protected special status in contrast to all other nations; it is a claim on Israel, a task given to it, because all the other nations are to learn to know the one and only God through this elect nation. It is through Israel and its behavior that the whole world will know God. Here is the dilemma to which Isaiah points at the beginning of his whole proclamation. If Israel no longer sees its duty and its task, fails to recognize its own origin as the elect nation, it not only cuts off its own tie to life, but even threatens to derail the natural order of things, which is God's order. In the election of Israel God has placed God's very self so much in human hands that God is no longer able to approach human beings at all if Israel separates itself and wants to be just another nation like all the others!

Hence the whole speech is only indirectly an accusation against Israel; in the first place it is an appeal to the whole world to recognize the significance of Israel's election for the world. This alone can lead to an encounter with the God who liberates and chooses, and thus gives and sustains life.

If we turn from this background in the words of Isaiah to the early Christian images of Christmas we quickly sense how many questions confront us in that familiar and cozy image of the child in the manger with the ox and ass. Do we recognize whom we encounter in this child in the manger, with the same simplicity and matter-of-factness, the same natural necessity, as the animal turns to its owner and its feedbox? Do we really understand that it is the God who liberated and chose Israel who comes to us here?

The owner, the master of the manger, whom the ox and ass recognize, is for Christians the God of Israel, and the manger itself, the feed box, can for them only be Israel's Bible, the so-called Old Testament. The image of the manger with the ox and ass thus quite clearly represents the continuity between the Old and New Covenants that so often goes unrecognized in the Christian world, a continuity that is based on the continuity of God's action. The lack of understanding shown by Israel's behavior, of which Isaiah speaks, thus passes as if by nature, in the early Christian image of Christmas, to the Christians, who do not want to recognize that continuity, or cannot. Marcion, the early heretic, who thought he must separate the Gods of the Old and New Testament because the one was a God of vengeance and the other a God of mercy, is an example from the early Church of just what such a Christmas image opposes.

The child in the manger, with ox and ass, is thus really anything but a mere depiction of the birth of Christ. It is a pictorial program that illuminates deep theological connections in order to make Christmas understandable for Christians in its true significance at last. Such a Christmas image represents a much more in-depth realization of the biblical message than our often banal question: "What does it mean for me?" The image with the ox and ass at the manger does not pose a lot of questions, but sets us, as viewers, in the middle of the event itself. The image asks us: What do you think of the so-called Old Covenant? Do you recognize the liberator of Israel in this child in the manger? Do you even guess what it means that "the LORD has spoken"?

Saint Jerome summarized the questions posed by this Christmas image in a few words: "Not to know Scripture is not to know Christ!" Christians have too often and too quickly misunderstood and banalized this saying by applying it to the New Testament, as if Jerome meant that those who do not know the New Testament can know nothing of Jesus the Christ. But Jerome's thinking was not so simple or so trivial. For his time "Scripture" was Israel's Bible, the later Old Testament of Christians. Only those who know it can, as Jerome understands the matter, also know Christ, because only on the basis of Scripture can one recognize that from Jesus' birth to his death and resurrection the God of Israel is revealed.

But Who Do You Say That I Am?

Sometimes I imagine a church congregation—or I wish for one—that would put up a Christmas crèche with only the ox and ass and the child in the manger. . . . As a Christmas sermon, the pastor would pass on to the (probably irritated) congregation all the questions this child in the manger poses to us: Who do you say that I am? Whom do you encounter in me? Do you know the children my heavenly Father reared and brought up? Do you know that I am lying in the manger so that you can understand that God has already said something to you through Israel, and that your Old Testament is meant to give you nourishment and life?

The answers to these questions, which each individual must give for himself or herself, lead us to the center of what Christmas is: encounter with God. What else can come from God's becoming human? Making an image of that encounter can never violate the biblical prohibition of making images, because it is not making an image of God to be venerated; it is solely a matter of showing the beginning of the Christ-event.

We have retained a tiny bit of the ancient image of Christmas, which was meant to point to something grand, in our great crèche landscapes with countless figures. We simply call all the scenes, those with spreading fields full of shepherds or Magi already starting out from their eastern lands and the tiniest portrayal of the Holy Family alone, "cribs" or "crèches." Thus we take as a designation for the whole thing the very word that the Church Fathers chose as a key to the joining of Old and New Testament in the interpretation of the Christmas message.

Is it not possible that just here, at Christmas, the biblical prohibition of images could take on a new meaning for us? For at the very moment when God appears, becomes visible in human form, we can comprehend that we must learn how to see pictures.

Joseph, What Are You Dreaming?

Christian piety has always depicted this Joseph, Mary's husband, as faithful and good, and in order to image Mary's virginity Christian art has often represented him as a kind of Methusaleh leaning on a staff next to the blooming young girl, Mary. However, that may only be a consequence of the fact that we know very little about this Joseph, for what the evangelists (and of them only Matthew and Luke) tell us about him is more than sparse. What was it, then, that brought about this strange image of Joseph? Is it Matthew's saying that Joseph was a righteous man and therefore wanted to dismiss Mary quietly? Or is it his unresisting obedience to the voice of the angel heard in his dream that has made this Joseph so colorless, merely an instrument for carrying out divine commands? But it may be just here, in Joseph's dream, that the deep misunderstanding leading to this image is lurking.

The first two chapters of Matthew's gospel tell of an angel of the Lord speaking to Joseph in a dream several times (Matt 1:20; 2:13, 19). Joseph always does exactly what he is told to do in the dream. He takes Mary as his wife, names the child she bears "Jesus," flees to Egypt to escape Herod, and returns after the king's death. He even has to be told in a dream where he should settle on his return, so he is ordered to Nazareth. The only decision Joseph himself makes in Matthew's infancy narrative, namely to dismiss Mary (Matt 1:19) is, according to the evangelist, wrong and in need of correction, and that is just what happens, right away, by means of the angel in the dream.

Are Dreams Only Shadows?

But doesn't the evangelist, who has such decisive turning points in his story take place in dreams, know that this medium, the dream, was regarded very skeptically and critically even in the Old Testament? Thus, for example, Jeremiah points out that prophets are emerging and claiming to have had a dream, but that God is personally opposed to this: "let the prophet who has a dream tell the dream" (Jer 23:28). The book of Job does admit that it is God who approaches a human being in a dream, but emphasizes a very different aspect of these dreams than does Matthew's gospel or the quotation from Jeremiah:

> For God speaks in one way,
>> and in two, though people do not perceive it.
> In a dream, in a visitation of the night,
>> when deep sleep falls on mortals,
>> while they slumber on their beds,
> then he opens their ears,
>> and terrifies them with warnings,
> that he may turn them aside from their deeds,
>> and keep them from pride,
> to spare their souls from the Pit,
>> their lives from traversing the River.
> They are also chastened with pain upon their beds,
>> and with continual strife in their bones. . . . (Job 33:14-19)

This seems to be more about nightmares, and the voice of God mentioned here appears to be the human conscience that speaks in the night. Finally, Qoheleth speaks critically of dreams, which for him represent the nothingness and mutability of all human life: ". . . dreams come with many cares" (Qoh 5:3) or "with many dreams come vanities and a multitude of words . . ." (Qoh 5:7). The book of Deuteronomy ultimately goes so far as to threaten death for dream-seers who are not in agreement with Israel's revealed word (Deuteronomy 13).

Looking to the Future

Of course, dreams are also seen differently in the Old Testament. Who will not immediately recall Daniel's interpretation of

Nebuchadnezzar's dream (Daniel 2), or Joseph's dream interpretations in Egypt (Genesis 40–41)? Those two great dream stories in the Old Testament witness to the great importance given to the interpretation of dreams in the whole Near East, for the story of Daniel takes place in Mesopotamia and that of Joseph in Egypt. In both places dreams are understood to be views of the human future, which—being thus recognized—can be influenced by appropriate magic rituals. For example, an Egyptian text says that "He (the god) has created medicines so that sickness may cease, and wine so that care may cease. He has created dreams to show their possessor the way he cannot see. He created for them (human beings) magic as a weapon to avert the blow of evil events and for the same purpose dreams at night and in the day."

But the evangelist Matthew, in his infancy gospel's narrative of Joseph, is not interested in dream images that require interpretation, and this Joseph is not given knowledge of his future through the dreams, as if they were to help in making decisions. Instead, through the medium of the dream he is told as bluntly as possible what he is to do. The evangelist would certainly have been aware of the skepticism about dreams in the Old Testament, but in his story it is not a question of revelations to be passed on to a group or to the whole people, as in the case of the prophets. This is solely about this Joseph and what he has to do. The principal problem the Old Testament traditions find in dreams is their strong individualism and the resulting difficulty of communicating images and messages received in dreams. But does that explain why the evangelist speaks of Joseph's dreams in such concentrated fashion?

Why Must Joseph Dream?

In these dreams of Joseph's there are two things that are especially evident. One is his *entry* into these dreams, which does not happen in sleep, but while he is still planning to dismiss Mary (Matt 1:20)—although at the end of the angel's message we read that Joseph awoke and did everything the angel had commanded him. In addition, we note that the other dream stories all have to do with a change of location: first from Bethlehem to Egypt, then back from Egypt, and finally to Nazareth. Is the evangelist using Joseph's dreams to give us a hint for understanding the story of Jesus? Doesn't this remind us of another person who learned of God's accompaniment on his path through messages given in dreams?

> Jacob left Beer-sheba and went toward Haran. He came to a certain place and stayed there for the night, because the sun had set. Taking one of the stones of the place, he put it under his head and lay down in that place. And he dreamed that there was a ladder set up on the earth, the top of it reaching to heaven; and the angels of God were ascending and descending on it. And the LORD stood beside him and said, "I am the LORD, the God of Abraham your father and the God of Isaac; the land on which you lie I will give to you and to your offspring; and your offspring shall be like the dust of the earth, and you shall spread abroad to the west and to the east and to the north and to the south; and all the families of the earth shall be blessed in you and in your offspring. Know that I am with you and will keep you wherever you go; and will bring you back to this land; for I will not leave you until I have done what I have promised you." Then Jacob woke from his sleep and said, "Surely the LORD is in this place—and I did not know it!" And he was afraid, and said, "How awesome is this place! This is none other than the house of God, and this is the gate of heaven." So Jacob rose early in the morning, and he took the stone that he had put under his head and set it up for a pillar and poured oil on the top of it. He called that place Bethel [the house of God]." (Gen 28:10-19)

Jacob had to go away to his mother's brother, as his parents wished, to take a wife from his own tribe. He moves into an uncertain future. Then comes the night event that will be decisive for the rest of his life. How close God is, and where God is nearest, is something Jacob does not know. An unprepossessing place, a stone, and then suddenly the certainty that God is there, unavoidable: Jacob is seized by this unexpected encounter with God. He calls the place "awesome." He may sense that his life has been fundamentally changed here, that great and difficult things will be demanded of him. He did not want to come so close to God, to meet God in this way. No, he knew nothing of that nearness; only the dream made it clear to him. Such an encounter, the deepest experience of God, cannot be achieved through human desire and planning; it always comes from divine initiative.

The later experiences of the people of Israel are concentrated, in anticipation, in the person of Jacob, who is here told that he must first leave the land but he will be brought back to it by God. In all this, God will be with him. For Jacob the promises of land and posterity made to Abraham (cf. Genesis 12) are here renewed. He, the later patriarch of the twelve tribes of Israel, becomes the symbol of all Israel, a fact that is indicated in the later event in which Jacob is renamed *Israel* (Gen 32:29; 35:10). Still, God's nearness does not remain limited to the dream, even though God's angel gives him advice in dreams (Gen 31:11). The story of Jacob's struggle at the Jabbok (Gen 32:23-33) clearly illustrates how he is seized and captured by God.

God Is Here

In his dream Jacob discovers the meaning of the place where he is. God breaks into Jacob's world, encounters him. With this dream about the ladder to heaven the biblical narrator introduces us readers to the significance of Jacob for the later people of Israel, who will be named for him.

And Joseph?

He also learns understanding through dreams. Of course he knows what is going on. Mary is pregnant (not by him), and he is considering her dismissal. But while he is still struggling with the facts of his life, with what he knows or thinks he knows, God's world breaks into his world in a dream. He, in fact, must confess as Jacob does: the LORD is here, and I did not know it. He does not say this, but we see that he recognizes it from the fact that he uncomplainingly does what the angel tells him. If Jacob anticipated the later destiny of Israel in his own person, namely having to leave the promised land in order to be led back there by God at a later time, so Joseph will ultimately have to accomplish the same thing in his own life, when the angel soon calls him to flee to Egypt with Mary and the child, and later to return.

Children of Israel

That Matthew really incorporates the core of Israel's faith, the Exodus, into this story is clear from the scriptural reference he inserts at the end of the story: "Out of Egypt I called my son" (Matt 1:15). It is true that this quotation comes from the book of Hosea (Hos 11:1), but even there it is a reference back to Israel's exodus from Egypt. The event to which the Jacob story looks forward is recalled in the story of Jesus' infancy and the role of Joseph. In both places it is the same God, Israel's liberator, who enters the world to be close to human beings through divine being-with. In the message of the dream Jacob receives a renewal of the promises already given to Abraham, and so becomes Israel's tribal ancestor. Through the reminiscence of Jacob at the beginning of the Gospel of Matthew, in the person of Joseph, all those who confess Jesus the Christ are reminded of their special union with Israel and Israel's promises. As little as Joseph is the physical father of Jesus, so little are all Christians physical members of the people of Israel; but in his dream Joseph is summoned, so to speak, to a spiritual fatherhood of this Jesus. Should not we Christians here discover, through this Joseph, our spiritual status as children: children of Jacob, children of Israel?

Behind this apparently modest story of Joseph's dreams is a powerful message from the evangelist. We learn only indirectly about Jacob through the story of his dream of the heavenly ladder. In the foreground stands the place itself. Beth-El, the house of God (the literal translation) is a sign that God descends, becoming concrete and perceptible in our human world.

We scarcely learn anything about Joseph, but his story, his dreams clarify for us, the readers of the gospel, that this Jesus represents a heavenly ladder, touching and uniting heaven and earth. Those who have eyes to see and ears to hear, these see and hear at the very beginning, with the birth of Jesus, the evangelist's message: Truly the LORD is here!

God Is Faithful

At first the message remains hidden, recalling the unknowing of Jacob and Joseph, but for readers of the gospel God is revealed more and more, bit by bit, in this Jesus. At the beginning of Jesus' story the God of Jacob meets us in Joseph's dreams, yet this is the same God whom Moses describes as "the God of Abraham, the God of Isaac, and the God of Jacob," and whom Moses and his people encounter as the God of liberation. In the stories of Joseph's dreams Matthew reminds us of this God whom we know from the written accounts of the experiences of the ancestors of Israel and the people delivered from Egypt.

No, this is no more a pious, nice little Christmas story than Joseph is a good, silent, obedient man standing at Mary's and Jesus' side. There is nothing less at stake here than God, God's faithfulness to Israel, God's promises to Israel. With the message of his *Christmas story* Matthew shifts us to a place where we encounter God. It is Israel's Bible, our Old Testament, where experiences of God and the history of the faith of generations are collected. When we hear the message of the Old Testament we often find ourselves, in the place of this encounter with God, like Jacob at Bethel, and we must confess: Truly the LORD is here, and I did not know it! Matthew addresses himself to this unknowing, because the birth of Jesus is a deed of Israel's savior.

Joseph at the manger stands for Israel's history with God and Israel's hopes, which Matthew recalls by placing a genealogy from Abraham to Joseph at the beginning of his gospel.

If Easter is the highest festival of Christianity and the beginning of the Christian faith, Christmas, by contrast, can be understood as the feast of God's faithfulness and our Christian unity with Israel. If we look at it in this way, in the truest sense of the word we discover that Joseph, standing at the manger, is Jacob: Israel, the tribal ancestor of the people of God. Then some of the psalmist's praise of the history of Israel reads like a Christmas carol:

> O give thanks to the LORD, call on his name,
>> make known his deeds among the peoples.
> Sing to him, sing praises to him;
>> tell of all his wonderful works.
> Glory in his holy name;
>> let the hearts of those who seek the LORD rejoice.

Seek the LORD and his strength;
>
> seek his presence continually.

Remember the wonderful works he has done,
>
> his miracles, and the judgments he uttered,

O offspring of his servant Abraham,
>
> children of Jacob, his chosen ones.

He is the LORD our God;
>
> his judgments are in all the earth.

He is mindful of his covenant forever,
>
> of the word that he commanded, for a thousand generations,

the covenant that he made with Abraham,
>
> his sworn promise to Isaac,

which he confirmed to Jacob as a statute,
>
> to Israel as an everlasting covenant. (Ps 105:1-10)

A New Era Begins

There used to be books published in Germany, in German, whose year of publication was given in the 5000s. That was not a science fiction projection, nor was it a printing error. It was a part of our culture that was ended by the Nazi reign of terror. Before that at least a few people were made aware, by such dates in books, that their Jewish fellow citizens calculated time in a different way. While the eras we were familiar with always had to be identified as *before* or *after Christ*, the Jewish calendar had no need of that. It was based on a reckoning of biblical chronology (from the creation of the world). According to that reckoning, in Advent 2000 we will be in the year 5760. Of course no one started a calendar at the beginning of the world and added to it every year, any more than anyone had the idea of beginning a new calendar as soon as Jesus was born.

It was in the third century of our era that someone first proposed a chronology beginning with the birth of Jesus. The well-traveled Christian Julius Africanus, a native of Jerusalem, developed this calendar after he had combined general dates from history with biblical events in a broad-scale work called a "Chronography." But why, we may ask, was there need for a new calendar? Was the existing one not adequate, or not exact enough?

Those who number their years *since the birth of Christ* show what it is by which they orient themselves and under whose lordship they stand, for the usual system of reckoning time in antiquity was oriented to the regnal years of the ruler. This led inevitably to a situation in which every dating announced adherence to a nation or the sphere of someone's rule. If we listen carefully, then, we must hear in our dating "after Christ," so much a matter of course for us, a confession of this Jesus, the Christ. But unlike the numbering according to regnal years, the Christian calendar is not restricted to the life and work of Jesus; it takes him simply as its starting point in order to determine all times from that one.

From the Beginning

This idea of a connected calendar stems from Jewish tradition, which also attempted to derive a calendar for the whole history of the world and humanity from the biblical accounts. To understand why Christianity conceived its own calendar beginning with Jesus Christ, and did not retain the Jewish calendar beginning with the creation of the world, one must look back to the very beginning, where the Jewish reckoning of time had its start, namely on the first page of the Bible, in the so-called first creation account.

> In the beginning when God created the heavens and the earth, the earth was a formless void and darkness covered the face of the deep, while a wind from God swept over the face of the waters. Then God said, "Let there be light"; and there was light. And God saw that the light was good; and God separated the light from the darkness. God called the light Day, and the darkness he called Night. And there was evening and there was morning, the first day. . . . And on the seventh day God finished the work that he had done, and he rested on the seventh day from all the work that he had done. So God blessed the seventh day and hallowed it, because on it God rested from all the work that he had done in creation. (Gen 1:1-5; 2:2-3)

God establishes a beginning. The first sentence of this text leaves us in no doubt that the author thinks of God as the universal creator. Accordingly, he does not begin his account of the beginning where later philosophical and theological traditions tried to establish such an idea, that is, with creation from nothing. No, the biblical author does not see creation as a gigantic miracle in which God conjures the material world out of nothing in the truest sense of the word. The modern question of the origins of matter was apparently of little interest to the biblical author; for him the miracle of creation lay rather in an order, an inherent lawfulness, that we can observe in Nature even though and precisely because God willed it this way and not otherwise in an eternity before time. To obtain an idea of the order of creation, the lawfulness of Nature, the author simply begins with its opposite, chaos, *tohuwabohu,* as the Hebrew text reads. Similarly, disorder is not to be thought of here as if everything were simply lying around and God merely had to tidy it up. No, God brings things forth and causes them to be, and first of all light, as the beginning so concisely states.

The Birth of Time

But what is this first day really about? Just light and darkness? Probably not, because God only creates light, while darkness is presumed and represents the original condition. But what is created is not *the* light that makes for life in the world, that is, the sun. From the perspective of this story it, together with the moon and stars, is created later (cf. Gen 1:14-19). The mention of a day and a night indicates, rather, that the creation of light aims at something else, namely the rhythm of day and night. This rhythm determines the course of time in the world, as the closing formula of the first day shows; it recurs then in the following six days of this story.

According to the first creation account, we should probably say, God creates time first of all. Time runs on continually and determines our whole life between arrival and departure. We are, indeed, subjected to it, inserted inescapably into the course of time and unable to influence it. However, the biblical narrator does not stop with this general statement about time as the fundamental category of the world and the human; within his *order of creation* he introduces a still broader concept, one that is provocative because it is *unnatural* and yet is depicted here as a part of the order of creation. I am referring to the division of time into weeks of seven days.

The Rhythm of Time

This seven-day week, constructed on the basic formula "six plus one," originated in Israel. It agrees with no natural order.

While the year, as a division of time, is oriented to the course of the sun and thus can be read from Nature, and the month, following the natural sequence of the moon's phases, is equally *natural,* the week as we know it represents an arbitrary ordinance. Ultimately it is the product of the Sabbath. The establishment of a day of rest that recurred every seven days as an identifying sign led, in Israel, to the unique system of a division of time into weeks in a rhythm of six work days and a day of rest. Two originally quite different institutions were thus combined: on the one hand the rhythm of "six plus one," known from the fallowing of land and similar customs even in antiquity, and on the other hand the Sabbath, previously known as a monthly feast day. The combination of the two ultimately led to a weekly Sabbath, that is, the recurrence of a Sabbath after six days, and thus indirectly to the establishment of the week as a unit of time, something that seems so matter of fact to us that we take it for granted. That was just what the biblical narrator had in mind when he made the seven-day plan, as a rhythm of "six plus one," the basis of his account of creation.

Nevertheless, it should be noted as regards the biblical presentation that there is no commandment in the creation story that obligates people to keep the Sabbath as a day of rest. It is simply stated that *God* adheres to this rhythm of time in establishing the order of our world. For human beings, however, this rhythm is at first unrecognizable, because it cannot be read directly from Nature.

The Miracle of the Seventh Day

If we continue to follow the biblical account, it takes a long time before the people of Israel are confronted with this rhythm of time. Only when they are constituted as God's people at Sinai, after God has been revealed to them, do they receive the Sabbath commandment as one part of the Decalogue (Exod 20:8-11). But anyone who has carefully read the stories in between has noticed that Israel is not entirely unprepared for this Sabbath commandment when it is received.

Immediately before their encounter with God at Sinai the people have grumbled and cried out to God because they are starving. But before the people's hunger drives them to a complete uprising against Moses, who led the people out of Egypt, the miracle occurs. Bread falls from heaven; something edible covers the ground like hoarfrost (Exodus 16). However, the lifesaving miracle has something special about it: this stuff spoils easily! It is only good for one day, and the next morning it has to be gathered again. With God one must often live from hand to mouth, no matter how much we long for security.

The happy ending of this biblical story of Israel's exodus from Egypt appears to be perfected in this miracle. But wait! The real miracle of the manna is yet to come. Unexpectedly and inexplicably, every six days bread falls that has an "expiration date" twice as long as the others, so that there need be no gathering on the seventh day and yet there will be something to eat. For us, who have internalized the rhythm of the week as a matter of course, the whole thing sounds perfectly normal and ordinary, because we fall into that rhythm in doing our weekend shopping on Saturday. But for those who have read the story of the Bible from the beginning, the special character of this passage emerges quite clearly. At the time of this manna miracle the people of Israel knows nothing yet about the seventh day, the Sabbath, and the rhythm of the week. It first learns from this remarkable bread that the seventh day is something special. Thus through a miracle Israel is prepared for the gift of time, the Sabbath.

A Light Shines

It is quite clear in Judaism to this day that the Sabbath recalls the fundamental order of all time since creation. At the beginning of the Sabbath a Jewish woman kindles the Sabbath light, just before sunset on Friday evening. In accord with the biblical formula "and there was evening and there was morning," every day ends with sunset and the next begins with evening. Against this background it is immediately obvious why the Jewish calendar begins with the *creation of the world.* Every week the Sabbath lights recall that God stands behind our entire life, since God is the origin of time and at the same time is the one who, through a revelation to

Israel, divides human time into small, visible units of weeks. Reckoning the whole time of the world from the creation means remembering our origins in God and living the experience of God's care for us.

God's care became concrete, according to Christian faith, in a unique form. God, this very God, became human in Jesus Christ! A new light dawns on the world. Jesus, the light of the world, shows us that God desires to save humanity, that God's care and concern for human beings is very human. The ancient and all-too-pious-sounding word "grace" means nothing else than this divine care and concern. Through Jesus, all human beings and all nations are to have a share in the nearness to God that was already the lot of Israel as God's elect people. The blessing spoken by a Jewish woman as she lights the Sabbath candles, "Blessed are you, Eternal God, Ruler of the World, who bless us with your commandments and command us to kindle the Sabbath lights," shows that these lights cause Israel's special calling to shine forth clearly; after all, it says "bless us with your commandments." In the same way, the Christmas lights remind us Christians of Jesus, the light of the world, who causes God's love to shine forth for all humanity.

God in Our Time

Christians, who begin counting all their time from Christ's coming into our world, thus confess Jesus as the light of the world. From that point of view the feast of Christmas is a new beginning, not only recalling the beginning of creation, but also a beginning in the rhythm of time. It is not a coincidence that Christians took over the rhythm of the week but transferred the day of celebration, the Sabbath, from the last to the first day of the week, so that their week has a rhythm of "one plus six." The birth of Christ, Christmas, is a gift of time that causes us to know that all is not simply in flux, but that the whole time of the world just as much as the short span of a human life has its rhythm. Even the two thousandth year *since the birth of Christ* recalls that God, who made our cosmos begin with time (Gen 1:2) came down and entered into this world of time. When we bless the first day of every week as a *Sabbath* and see in Christ's birth the beginning of a new era, Christmas must become a nodal point or an "island in time," as a rabbi called the Sabbath.

Even though the new Church year has already begun, and especially because our earthly year shifts a few days after Christmas, we can experience Christmas as a festival of the time God gives us. It is not a time to be "killed" or used up with more and more activities, but a time that exists for us to internalize God's time, from creation to consummation. The recollection of the Christian reckoning of time *since the birth of Christ* draws our gaze to the beginning, the creation of the world, and thus to our origin. And is that origin not also a pointer to our goal?

How often do we write the number of the year in the course of three hundred sixty-five days, without adding "since the birth of Christ," without stopping once to think that a date formulated in that way is meant to remind us of God's history with us humans? The birth of Christ as a starting point for calculating time does not allow us to forget that there was a time *before the birth of Christ* and not only *since the birth of Christ*. What is special here can perhaps be sensed if we deliberately think of the difference between a Jewish and a Christian time-reckoning by emphasizing that Jesus the Jew was born in the year 3760 according to the Jewish calendar. Not everything begins anew; time simply goes on; but God's grace, God's care for us, is newly perceptible to us. Christmas people are those who are always beginning anew, because they know that there is someone who has already begun with and for them, in creation as well as in the birth of Jesus.

If God can *begin* something with us because we do not use God's time simply as a means of calculation, then truly *a new era can begin!*

In Order That Might Be Fulfilled . . .

A man wakes up in the morning, and the day begins as usual . . . and that happens over and over as if time had stopped and never moved beyond that one day. A comedy film, "Groundhog Day," forces on us the unbearable thought of the eternal return. What makes the film so funny is something that really touches us very deeply. We would like to find some way to counter the simple course of time so as to avoid eternal sameness. All our hopes and expectations, great and small, ultimately aim at effecting change in the course of ever-returning time. And yet we live from the fact that the recurring course of time is always filled differently and anew for and with us.

A word from the prophet Jeremiah touches just this nerve; it pleads for attention to the time to come: "The days are surely coming, says the LORD" (Jer 33:14). To the obvious question—what will be so special about these days that the prophet announces, what will fill that time?—the text points simply to a saving word that God had already spoken to Israel: "when I will fulfill the promise I made to the house of Israel and the house of Judah" (Jer 33:14). Readers of the book of Jeremiah have little trouble discovering what the prophet is here referring to, because shortly before the section thus introduced we find a major section of text in the book of Jeremiah, called the "book of consolation" because it speaks of the changes in the eternal sameness that God will bring for Israel. A number of strophes in that book of consolation begin with the same introductory words: "the days are surely coming, says the LORD" (Jer 30:3; 31:27, 31). But the change that God announces to God's people, who are living in Babylonian exile, by saying that God will alter the fate of God's people, does not consist in something absolutely new, something that has never happened before, but in the making-effective of what God has always promised, from the time of Abraham: life in the promised land, becoming a great nation, being in covenant with God. Because God forgives guilt and thinks no more of sins the book of consolation can announce a new covenant between God and Israel. That covenant itself is not new and is no other than the previous covenant, but God gives it in a different way so that people can no longer break it, with a new immediacy; God will place the Torah, God's commandments, within it and write it on their hearts (Jer 31:31-34).

Promise and Covenant

It is not as if God continually wanted to make new and different covenants, one with Noah, one with Abraham, one with Moses. . . . No, God is faithful, but God is also prepared to accommodate the covenant to people and their abilities; that is the only reason why God makes this one and only and eternally enduring covenant new and different. The book of Jeremiah reminds us of this fidelity in urgent fashion. If we read on, after the initial "the days are surely coming," we hear how God stands fast to the covenant. The text chooses time, in its unchanging endurance, as an image for this divine fidelity. "If any of you could break my covenant with the day and my covenant with the night, so that day and night would not come at their appointed time, only then could my covenant with my servant David be broken ..." (Jer 33:20-21). But when did God enter into a covenant with the day and with the night? The question one poses to oneself in view of this strange-sounding formulation is answered by reference to the very first covenant mentioned in the Bible. That is the covenant God made with Noah after the Flood. As a sign of the eternal divine covenant God placed a bow in the clouds, after having promised that day and night would never cease. As steady and unalterable as time, from which there is no escape, so are God's promises!

Precisely from this idea in the book of Jeremiah of a new covenant we Christians have all too often derived the misunderstanding that God's promise to human beings is subjected to the changes that fill the inexorable course of time. We think that God once made a covenant with Israel, and then a new and different one with us Christians, that God announced something through the prophets that was then fulfilled in Jesus. And especially in Advent and at Christmas we think all too often and all too fast in these categories of our human time, that God's promises must one day come to an end, to their fulfillment, as we say. When we Christians speak of what has been fulfilled in Jesus, of what is promised in the Old Testament, it often sounds a little like yesterday's weather report. What was predicted has happened or not, but in any case the announcement is taken care of, it is out of date, it has been fulfilled or not.

The fact that the biblical understanding of fulfillment, and thus also of promise, is quite different is shown by the Jeremiah text already cited, which says (in v. 14) that God will "fulfill" the promise made to Israel and Judah. But in the underlying Hebrew text the word translated "fulfilled" is a verb that means "set up, establish," and some Jewish translators deliberately translate it very literally, probably because of the Christian misunderstanding: for example, Martin Buber writes "I will see established the good word that I have spoken," or Leopold Zunz: "and I will maintain the good promise that I made."

Thus promises are not done with when they are fulfilled; they remain as promises, are *maintained* as promises; indeed they emerge, arise, and thus their *status* can be recognized. We Christians do not believe, after all, that the promise of the Messiah from Israel's Bible and its awaiting a redeemer were fulfilled in Jesus of Nazareth and his birth, that we remember at Christmas, in such a way that all the messianic hopes of the Bible are taken care of and our salvation is accomplished.

A Necessary Backward Glance

From this very point of view it is rewarding and helpful to take a closer look at the references to Israel's Bible that are often designated as "fulfillment quotations." The five explicit references contained in the "Christmas story" in Matthew's gospel point the way to the understanding of the link between the proclamation of Christ and the Bible of Israel in early Christianity.

The key word *fulfillment* appears in the very first citation in the New Testament: "All this took place to fulfill what had been spoken by the Lord through the prophet: 'Look, the virgin shall conceive and bear a son, and they shall name him Emmanuel,' which means, 'God is with us'" (Matt 1:22-23).

But it is utterly clear here that fulfillment has *nothing* to do with the idea that what was predicted has now been fully taken care of because it has happened. This is obvious both from the choice of words and from the way the content of the quotation is incorporated in the context. The word Matthew chooses for "fulfill" *(plēroō)* does not contain the aspect of "being finished with," or anything like that; it means "bring into effect" or "realize." The way Matthew uses the quotation underscores this, for with it Matthew looks back to the tense relationship between judgment and salvation in the story of the unbelief of King Ahaz in Isaiah 7. Anyone who is inspired by Isa 7:14 to read the whole story in Isaiah 7 and *projects* it into the context of Matthew 1 will first of all grasp the existential question posed by the interpretive verse from the Isaiah pericope in light of Matthew's proclamation of the Christ: "If you do not stand firm in faith, you shall not stand at all" (Isa 7:9). Then, however, the evangelist employs the quotation from Isa 7:14 to set an arch over his entire gospel, binding beginning to end. It is created by the difference of names between Jesus and Immanuel, which at the very beginning makes it clear that fulfillment has nothing to do with the setting of a mathematical equation. The promise in the book of Isaiah that he will be given the name Immanuel is not fulfilled in the narrow sense of the word; only in the last sentence of the gospel of Matthew is this great tension resolved when the Risen One (with the same introductory "Look!" as in Isa 7:14) tells his disciples" "I am with you" (Matt 28:20). Thus is the "God with us" of Matt 1:23, the "Emmanuel," explained, clarifying the literal translation of the name as well. In Matthew's perspective, then, the promise of Immanuel is not *fulfilled* in Jesus' birth, but it becomes effective in that event and is verified in what follows, as a promise beyond Jesus' death and resurrection.

The second quotation that Matthew inserts from Israel's Bible is incorporated in the story with a great degree of narrative skill, for in Matt 2:5-6 Matthew has the scribes answer Herod's question about the place where the Messiah is to be born with a citation from Scripture: "They told him, 'In Bethlehem of Judea; for so it has been written by the prophet: *And you, Bethlehem . . .*'" (Matt 2:5-6). If even here, where it seems so appropriate in the sense of a "scriptural proof," Matthew does *not* speak of "fulfillment" of Scripture, as we hastily and superficially presuppose to be the case with all scriptural quotations, it ought to give us pause for thought.

The third quotation Matthew uses makes it quite clear that what was promised has been realized. If we read the little episode of the flight into Egypt (Matt 2:13-15) without an agenda we have the impression that this strange journey is only reported in order to give occasion for the concluding quotation from Hosea 11: "Out of Egypt I have called my son." Through this quotation the magnificent poem about God's fidelity and love toward Israel in Hosea 11 is "woven into" the narrative. Matthew employs the recollection of the exodus from Egypt that is involved, the sign of God's love, to make it clear at the beginning of his gospel that in this Jesus the liberator God of the Exodus, who loves Israel, is speaking. When Matthew here speaks of the fulfillment of the prophetic word this can only be understood as the verification of the experience of God that happened in the Exodus.

In the next citation, the fourth, Matthew does not use the final form "in order that might be fulfilled," but the statement form: "Then was fulfilled. . . ." Matthew's intention is not to present the slaughter of the innocents under the heading of "promise and fulfillment," but to use the quotation to help his readers and hearers understand the story of Jesus as a whole. The quotation about Rachel's weeping and lamenting in Ramah is from Jeremiah, more precisely from Jer 31:15, the book of consolation we mentioned earlier. There will be another recollection of the book of consolation in Jeremiah at the end of the gospel, when Jesus, as he blesses the cup, speaks of the blood of the covenant that will be shed for many for the forgiveness of sins (Matt 26:28; cf. Jer 31:31, 34). In contrasting the death of many for the one with the death of the one for many Matthew interprets the drama of the Christ-event on the basis of the Bible of Israel.

The last of the five quotations, finally, leads us to the foundation of them all, namely the general authority of Scripture in early Christianity. Matthew associates the information that Joseph, following instructions received in a dream, settles with his family in Nazareth with a "fulfillment reference" to "the prophets" who said "He will be called a Nazorean" (Matt 2:23). There is no such reference in any of the prophets of Israel's Bible or in any other Old Testament book. There have been many attempts to refer the quotation to similar-sounding Hebrew words, but that is really no help, because the association with the place, Nazareth, is constitutive for the pericope Matt 2:19-23, and in addition, Christians were familiar with the title "Nazorean." Here we have a scriptural reference that is not based on any clearly evident scriptural passage. Something like it is found in one of the oldest Christian confessions, handed on and quoted by Paul in 1 Cor 15:4: "and that he was buried, and that he was raised on the third day in accordance with the scriptures." There is no biblical passage that speaks of resurrection on the third day. Such scriptural references express "the faith conviction of something having been willed by God" (Franz Mußner). By reference to the Bible—"the prophets" in early Christianity could represent the whole of Scripture (cf. Heb 1:1)—emphasis is placed on the agreement of the account with God's revelation. For Matthew that is of an importance not to be underestimated as he closes his infancy gospel; this statement, which appears somewhat marginal, seems rather like a summary of Christian conviction regarding Israel's Bible that can be developed in the further accounts of the gospel.

Our very everyday Christianity—in the course of time—could, however, move into an entirely different space if we would surrender ourselves to this "fulfillment" that Matthew presents to us so persistently at the very beginning of his gospel. Since Jesus' birth our times have been filled and fulfilled with God's promises, contained so richly in our Old Testament, the Bible of Israel.

In Our Midst

In the nineteenth century, when the remains of a medieval wall painting of portions of the book of Ezekiel were discovered in a small church in the Rhineland, a small anomaly appeared. Besides the depiction of a city gate, within which there was a figure of Christ, the restorer attempted to reconstruct a figure of Mary out of the few lines that were still discernible. The reason for this was the appearance of two words in small letters below the border of the picture: MARIA SACRA. In the context of the images from the book of Ezekiel depicted there the association between the picture and Mary was easy to understand, even without a specific image of Mary, for the scene referred to the so-called closed Eastern gate of the new Jerusalem in Ezekiel 44, which in turn is part of the great cycle of visions in the book of Ezekiel.

He Departs and Returns Again

In the call vision at the beginning of the book (Ezekiel 1–3) the prophet sees that the glory of the Lord is mobile, and is not fixed at the location of the temple, in the Holy of Holies. He understands the meaning of this strange vision later when, in another vision (Ezekiel 8–11), he is shown the sins and evil deeds of Jerusalem, and he sees how the glory of the Lord leaves the city before the approaching judgment of destruction. Later the prophet Ezekiel receives an insight, in the truest sense of the word, into the new Jerusalem (Ezekiel 40–48). In another magnificent vision he is shown the outermost Eastern gate of the sanctuary, which was closed and is to remain so because God, who previously had departed from the city, has returned through it. Ezekiel's visions are characteristically concrete. Everything the prophet sees of this new Jerusalem, often called "heavenly," is described to the millimeter. The purpose of these almost tiresomely detailed descriptions is to show that the prophet has not received private revelations, nor does he proclaim secret religious mysteries; in the vision he has been given a message for God's people, and he must hold precisely to what he has seen in order to pass it on.

The Sealed Gate

But all that he sees of this new Jerusalem does not end with his perception and description of the city in all its details. The city does not remain a dead place of ghosts; no, it is filled with life, and that life comes primarily from the fact that God, the source of all life, enters into the city. The sealed gate refers to this core idea. A sealed gate has surrendered its original and proper function: it no longer gives access. Having become almost identical with the rest of the wall, it nevertheless poses questions to the viewer, precisely because it is a sealed gate. Why is it sealed? Has someone seeking protection sealed it up? Are others shut out from what is happening behind the walls? Or is it undesirable that people should go in and out at this place? The answer to these questions posed by the sealed gate is given with clear precision by the book of Ezekiel: "This gate shall remain shut; it shall not be opened, and no one shall enter by it; for the LORD, the God of Israel, has entered by it; therefore it shall remain shut" (Ezek 44:2). The fixed and unchangeable character of the sealed gate is thus meant to recall something utterly living and dynamic. God has taken possession of this city and made it the place of divine presence. The sealed gate points like a signpost to the special character of the place. The last sentence in the book of Ezekiel formulates this idea then, finally, by saying that the name of this new city shall henceforth be: "The LORD is there" (Ezek 48:35). That is the program for the new Jerusalem; there is no longer a holy place somewhere or other, for God's very self fills the whole city, sanctifies it to the tiniest corner simply by being present. There is something terrifying in this idea that the unimaginable and all-powerful God is brought into such close union with what is particular and unavoidable for us humans, the limitations of space.

God in the World

Ezekiel's new Jerusalem, the city "The LORD is there," is provocative: God's very self descends into the human, into space and time, in order to fill everything there with divine glory. Not only have artists of all ages been inspired by these texts; so have mystics and visionaries of the most diverse kinds. Who can be surprised if the Church fathers themselves were reminded by this idea of *God in the world* of the Incarnation, God's becoming human in Jesus Christ?

In this perspective we find very early in Christianity, first with Ambrose of Milan in the fourth century, a Marian interpretation of this passage in Ezekiel about the sealed gate. The closed gate through which God has entered is seen as a reference to Mary's virginity. Are we then confronted with a Christmas image in the middle of the book of Ezekiel? In a certain sense we are, especially when we make this interpretation of the sealed gate a portal by which we enter into the depth of the prophet Ezekiel's thought. That is the only sense of a Marian interpretation, because a too-simple transfer to the notion of virginity contradicts the image itself: the Eastern gate in Ezekiel's vision is open until the glory of the Lord passes through it (Ezekiel 43); only then is it closed! The Marian interpretation of the passage thus only gives the impulse for reading the magnificence of Ezekiel's proclamation of the new Jerusalem as a question regarding the presence of God in our world. That was probably the idea of the medieval artist who painted the Ezekiel cycle mentioned above as well, when with the two words MARIA SACRA under the last picture in his series, the one devoted to the sealed gate, he pointed to the Christian interpretation of the passage. It is interesting, however, that he did not incorporate the interpretation in the picture itself (for example, by depicting Mary), but referred to it in the margin by adding a caption to the picture.

Holiness in Motion

If the image of the sealed gate from Ezekiel's vision and its
early Christian interpretation makes us think first of all of *Christmas imagery* in this prophetic book from the Old Testament,
which as a whole plays a very marginal role in the Church's liturgical tradition, and beyond that is scarcely ever connected with
messianic promises in Christian interpretation, we will swiftly
discover the great riches of the book. Like the treasure in the field,
they do not lie on the surface, but must be sought in its depths. In
the midst of the truly architectonic descriptions of this new city,
and following on the promise of the return of the Lord, we find in
Ezekiel a wonderful image full of movement and life, one that
makes the ideas we have already considered still more profound.

> Then he brought me back to the entrance of the temple; there,
> water was flowing from below the threshold of the temple toward
> the east (for the temple faced east); and the water was flowing
> down from below the south end of the threshold of the temple,
> south of the altar. Then he brought me out by way of the north
> gate, and led me around on the outside to the outer gate that faces
> toward the east; and the water was coming out on the south side.
>
> Going on eastward with a cord in his hand, the man measured
> one thousand cubits, and then led me through the water; and it
> was ankle-deep. Again he measured one thousand, and led me
> through the water; and it was knee-deep. Again he measured one
> thousand, and led me through the water; and it was up to the
> waist. Again he measured one thousand, and it was a river that I
> could not cross, for the water had risen; it was deep enough to
> swim in, a river that could not be crossed. He said to me, "Mortal,
> have you seen this?"
>
> Then he led me back along the bank of the river. As I came back,
> I saw on the bank of the river a great many trees on the one side
> and on the other. He said to me, "This water flows toward the east-
> ern region and goes down into the Arabah; and when it enters the
> sea, the sea of stagnant waters, the water will become fresh. Wher-
> ever the river goes, every living creature that swarms will live, and
> there will be very many fish, once these waters reach there. It will
> become fresh; and everything will live where the river goes. People
> will stand fishing beside the sea from En-gedi to En-eglaim; it will
> be a place for the spreading of nets; its fish will be of a great many

kinds, like the fish of the Great Sea. But its swamps and marshes will not become fresh; they are to be left for salt. On the banks, on both sides of the river, there will grow all kinds of trees for food. Their leaves will not wither nor their fruit fail, but they will bear fresh fruit every month, because the water for them flows from the sanctuary. Their fruit will be for food, and their leaves for healing." (Ezek 47:1-12)

It is an eloquent image, one that addresses the reader or hearer who surrenders to its visual power. The question posed to the prophet: "Mortal, have you seen this?" (Ezek 47:6) is addressed also to the hearers and readers, to us. Water comes forth from the innermost part of the temple and flows out over the land. A sanctuary no longer guards its holiness, but releases it into the world as healing water. There it brings growth and fullness and still more; it flows out to the farthest withering and dying place and gives it new life.

Dead Water Is Now Living

In order to appreciate the vivid power of this image one must know and have experienced the so-called Dead Sea, not far from Jerusalem in the Jordan valley. In the dry desert regions of the Near East water is *the* symbol of life. But water that, because of its high salt content, no longer sustains life, even rejects it, is itself dead— such water is loathsome. Still more: this water from the Dead Sea even seems to destroy the good, living water, for day by day the Jordan or, for example, the springs of the En-gedi bring sweet water into this sea, where it only evaporates and leaves crusts of salt on the shore. In Ezekiel's vision this experience is taken up and turned on its head. The water from the temple flows out into the land, becomes a roaring current, brings fruitfulness and life, and even in the Dead Sea its life-giving power does not fail; instead, this water causes even the Dead Sea to be converted into something living, in the truest sense of the words. There can scarcely be a more forceful description of the power of living water.

However, this healing and life-giving effect is only one side of Ezekiel's picture. It is not a water-filled river or a brimming spring that breaks out from the temple; the water simply trickles slowly down the temple wall. But outside the temple this trickle becomes a greater and greater stream. The prophet must experience this rising of the water over and over again in his own body. There is something about this water from the temple! Rapidly, the insignificant trickle from the temple becomes a powerful stream. What began so small—but in the place where God is nearest—becomes greater and greater, stronger and stronger, and the farther it flows into the land the more it vivifies everything it touches, because it remains connected to the insignificant-looking and yet not unimportant source in the inmost part of the sanctuary.

Our faith, hope, and love—or we may call them simply, in ancient terms, holiness—are often nothing but a tiny trickle when the church walls are behind us . . . but as long as it remains connected to the source there is a mighty power slumbering in that insignificant-appearing thing. In fact, new life is budding within it. Ezekiel gives another especially powerful expression to this slumbering power at the end of his pictorial description: trees whose leaves do not wither, and that produce fruit continually, month after month, grow on the banks of this water. This image of the tree appears also in Psalm 1 and in Jer 17:8, there as an image for people who trust entirely in God, rejoice in the Torah, and meditate on it day and night (Ps 1:2); such a person is like just such a tree.

By Their Fruits You Will Know Them

Trees like this are also the clearest sign of connection with God. Ezekiel drives this image to the limit. The Holy in the sanctuary comes into the world; it is an irresistible power of life that touches and fulfills everything. This power of God extends everywhere; nothing can resist it, not even the life-resistant Dead Sea.

The text offers two important indications that this image should not be seen in isolation and alone, but belongs in the larger context of Ezekiel's vision of the new Jerusalem. On the one hand there is the figure who accompanies the prophet, who three times measures a thousand cubits in order to illustrate to the prophet what power the stream has. This kind of measurement, which sharpens the prophet's eye for detail, already appeared several times in the inspection and touring of the new city and the temple. On the other hand there is the figure's question: "Mortal, have you seen this?" (Ezek 47:6), already proposed to the prophet more than once to call his attention to the significance of the things he sees in his visions. He, the prophet, is a human being—the word "mortal" in Hebrew emphasizes and underscores the idea of humanity—who receives an insight into the divine world. After the prophet has seen the concept of holiness for the new city and the temple in what is almost a "theology for architects" the image changes, from the static conception of the city to the dynamic of the divine in the vision of the temple water source. If the prophet has already seen how the glory of the Lord entered into this city and filled it to the fullest with divine holiness, the power of God's presence is now made clearer to him. God's presence here can no longer be limited, no longer fixed to the place of God's temple. It emerges, is perceptible as a power that awakens life in every place. The so-called heavenly Jerusalem of Ezekiel's vision is not a distant, world-alienated place, but a beginning of new life, of divine presence that comes to meet us human beings.

God in our midst!

What do we see, experience, and celebrate when Christmas is near?—the presence of God in the world, in a human being: God in our midst? Does the feast of Christ's birth, the appearance of the Lord, change something in us, as does the water from the temple fount that gives life to the whole land? Does Christmas really make us people joined to God who stand like trees on the banks of streams, whose foliage never fades because their roots reach deep into the water, and that produce abundant fruit?

The Marian interpretation of the sealed gate from Ezekiel's vision, which seems so strange to us, cannot, after all, be so quickly set aside as the relic of an outdated method of scriptural interpretation, for beneath the surface it conceals a more powerful impulse to a deeper understanding of the Christmas feast and the mystery of the birth of Christ than one suspects at first glance. The prophet Ezekiel, so little heard and so often forgotten in Christianity, leads us with open eyes to the sources of our faith: to the place where God is made visible in a *mortal human being.*

Yad Vashem

"O God, that Thou might remember the faith of our ancestors and bring their descendants a Savior for the sake of Thy Name and Thy lovingkindness."

This sounds a little like a prayer text from a Christmas liturgy, as if one were to reformulate the beginning of the Gospel of Matthew, the so-called "genealogy of Jesus," which begins "an account of the genealogy of Jesus the Messiah, the son of David, the son of Abraham" (Matt 1:1), as the basic idea of a prayer of petition. But the verse I have cited is not from a Christmas liturgy; it comes from the beginning of the Jewish liturgy for the Day of Atonement, Yom Kippur. As the cited text indicates, there is a close connection between this highest Jewish feast day and the Christian feast of Christmas.

The Feast of Our Redemption—The Day of Atonement

Central to the Jewish Day of Atonement are forgiveness, atonement, and reconciliation with God, as described in Leviticus 16. This fundamental idea is also found again and again in the Christmas liturgies, not only where Christmas is described as "the feast of our redemption," but even in the Alleluia verse for Christmas Eve, before the Gospel: "Tomorrow the wickedness of the earth will be destroyed: the Savior of the world will reign over us." The prayers for the day of Christmas also sound like texts from the Day of Atonement: they ask that God will give us reconciliation and join us together with God again, just as the Jewish liturgy, during the eight days of penitence that precede the Day of

Atonement, also lays great emphasis on the idea that reconciliation between God and the human being cannot be separated from the reconciliation of people with one another. The Mishnah says of this: "The Day of Atonement forgives sins between the human being and God; the Day of Atonement only forgives sins between a human being and his or her neighbor if he or she has made peace with that neighbor." Would not our Christmas joy, so richly shared in Christmas gifts, the expression of our consciousness of the gift of redemption received in the Incarnation, receive an even deeper meaning if we connected it to the idea of reconciliation, which is also proper to the feast of Christmas? A Christmas gift so consciously presented can only be given if it reflects reconciliation and mutual unity among human persons as an expression of reconciliation with God.

Memory Unites

The spiritual and theological ties between the Day of Atonement and Christmas can be mined still more deeply. A concept of hope is especially important for our understanding of Christmas. Israel's faith, as represented by the great figures of the Bible, constitutes the core of hope also, and especially, in the Jewish Day of Atonement, as the prayer text quoted at the beginning shows. Memory is the key word in this potential hope. First God is reminded of Israel's faith ("remember the faith of our ancestors"), and then the community and each individual remembers the history of God with God's people. Israel, it is often said, and rightly so, is the people of memory. Memory unites, creates identity, self-awareness, a consciousness and indeed a knowledge of who one is, where one comes from, what and for what one is. Those who know where they belong, where they come from, also know where they must go.

Those who no longer remember, those who forget—these tear up their own roots. And those who forget not only injure themselves, but also those they forget, those they no longer desire to remember. A Jewish saying expresses this quite brutally, but also very clearly: "Refusing to remember is murder!"

Refusing to remember is murder. Against it can stand only the most natural and best memory of a person, which happens in the continuing life of his or her own children.

In the course of its history the Jewish people all too often had to recognize and to learn that this most natural mode of human memory and continuing life can become impossible. Being murdered, driven out, scattered—these were only the external signs of internal damage and danger.

After the Babylonian exile the Jewish community found that not everyone could experience the natural ties of parents and children as incorporation into the community of faith. New people came who wanted to be Jews, but who had no genealogical roots in the Jewish community that they could remember. There were childless people who feared being forgotten because no one would remember them after their death. A text from that period, found in the third part of the book of Isaiah, clearly expresses the great difficulties thus experienced, and what God had to say about all this:

> Do not let the foreigner joined to the LORD say,
>> "The LORD will surely separate me from his people";
> and do not let the eunuch say,
>> "I am just a dry tree."
> For thus says the LORD:
> "To the eunuchs who keep my sabbaths,
>> who choose the things that please me
>> and hold fast my covenant,
> I will give, in my house and within my walls,
>> a monument and a name
>> better than sons and daughters;
> I will give them an everlasting name
>> that shall not be cut off." (Isa 56:3-5)

Thus God promises those who are fearful about their own memory, and thus their incorporation within the people of God, that God will personally erect a memorial to them, set up a "monument" (the text literally says that God will give them "a hand and a name"): as the Jewish religious philosopher Martin Buber translates it in his well-known *Yad Vashem*, "a sign, a monumental name." Love for the Torah and for God will inscribe these people in God's eternal covenant with Israel, which God, too, remembers, and that is always remembered where the people of God live and remember their history and their origin.

A Liberating God

The evangelist Matthew, whose work opens the New Testament and whose message is directed to those who, like the foreigners in the Isaiah text, are "joined to the Lord," that is, people who have joined Israel—this Matthew immediately reminds the hearers and readers of his gospel of the beginning. He opens his gospel with a genealogy. He writes the fathers and mothers of Israel into the family tree of Christians, as an abiding memory for them. Thus he describes the identity of Christians by establishing their connection, in memory, to the people of Israel, the people of God, because Jesus the Christ is a son of David, a son of Abraham. But that is not all. Matthew uses two little stories, episodes, or simply motifs to induct the Christians who hear or read his gospel into Israel's community of memory from the very start.

Because Herod has learned of the birth of the Anointed One of Israel, the Messiah, the parents must flee with the newborn child; with him and for his sake they are snatched away, loosed from all ties: ultimately, they are homeless. But in Matthew's story this flight has a purpose: "This was to fulfill what had been spoken by the Lord through the prophet, 'Out of Egypt I have called my son'" (Matt 2:15).

This last sentence, the prophetic word, comes from the book of Hosea, where it introduces one of the central texts of the book. Hosea 11 speaks of judgment and love. It describes how consistently and righteously, indeed necessarily, judgment must follow Israel's rebellious behavior. Yet at the end of the section God's wrathful judgment is completely overturned, and divine love for Israel gains the upper hand. "How can I give you up, Ephraim? How can I hand you over, O Israel?" (Hos 11:8). This is the uncontrollable love and mercy of God, contrary to all human logic, that shows us what God's being God means. This humanly unimaginable surplus of divine mercy has marked a great many central Old Testament faith-statements, and it is present everywhere in Jesus' preaching as well. In Hosea 11 this idea of the mercy of God is introduced by a look back at the beginnings of God's love affair with Israel. "When Israel was a child, I loved him, and out of Egypt I called my son" (Hos 11:1). Here, so to speak, the liberating deed of the Exodus is portrayed as a first act of love, a sign of "God in love." It is this memory of the Exodus that should make us see God's love that can never abandon Israel. Anyone in Israel who speaks of Egypt and Exodus and remembers them lives in hope of the endless love of God. Even after Hosea's day, in the time of the Babylonian exile, the memory of the Exodus was repeatedly awakened and spoken, and the evangelist Matthew also shows how this memory and hope were alive in Israel: the hope that God would again intervene to liberate and to gather the scattered people of Israel. For Matthew this is already to be seen in Jesus, from the beginning—at his birth—like a bud in spring. The little story about the flight into Egypt places this gospel, from the beginning, under the sign of the potential for hope inherent in the theology of exodus.

A New Covenant?

As a second motif, Matthew then presents Jesus' living contemporaries, his brothers among the people, so to speak: the baby boys of Bethlehem. They, who could carry on the name of God and the name of Israel and keep memory alive, are murdered because there is someone who is unwilling that the people of Israel should retain and keep alive the memory of God, its liberator, redeemer, and king. Children must die so that they can have no more children whom they can instruct about the expectation of Israel's Messiah. Hitler, like Herod, not only wanted to rub out the Jews, but also the memory of what they proclaim and witness to the world.

Matthew interprets this event in a way that seems cruel at first glance, because here, as in many other places, he inserts a "fulfillment quotation," as if what is reported here were part of God's plan of salvation. But it may be that a closer look at this "quotation" can shed some light on the meaning of the so-called "fulfillment quotations" as a group.

With the note that this fulfilled what was said by the prophet Jeremiah, Matthew quotes: "'A voice was heard in Ramah, wailing and loud lamentation, Rachel weeping for her children; she refused to be consoled, because they are no more'" (Matt 2:18; cf. Jer 31:15). Here it is abundantly clear that Matthew does not suppose there was a prophecy that was "fulfilled" in the slaughter of the innocents in Bethlehem. Instead, he intends that the quotation will serve as a key for his hearers and readers because they know where it comes from, and that they can recall, and indeed apply the larger context of the quotation to their understanding of the story of the murder of children in Bethlehem.

The verse comes from the so-called "book of consolation" in the book of the prophet Jeremiah, which offers consolation and hope to the exiles in its promise of the restoration of Israel. This whole promise is divided into three parts, each introduced by the words, "The days are surely coming, says the LORD" (Jer 30:3; 31:27, 31). After this introduction, in the first strophe the promise of the possession of the land, already given to the ancestors of Israel, is renewed: God promises to alter Israel's fate and bring the people back into the land. The second strophe, in the image of God's great sowing of seed, takes up the promise, also given to the ancestors, that Israel will increase and become a great nation. Finally, the passage culminates in the third strophe, which speaks of God's covenant with Israel and climaxes with the promise of a "new covenant." This new covenant promised in Jer 31:31 is not "new" in the sense of being a different covenant in contrast to the "old" one. Rather, God gives the one and only covenant of God with Israel, but in a new way. So that Israel can never again break the covenant, it is given a new immediacy. The Torah is written on Israel's heart. When God's instruction is so placed in the inmost heart of the human being, he or she can choose to do what pleases God, as the text cited above from Isaiah 56 says. However, the basis of all these promises of land, posterity, and new covenant is what is said at the very end: "for I will forgive their iniquity, and remember their sin no more" (Jer 31:34).

For Matthew, what is important in this little story at the very beginning of his gospel is the reference to the new covenant that is alluded to through the quotation. His message is grounded in the memory of unconsolable Rachel, the history of the suffering of the people whom God will nevertheless console and liberate. With these two stories Matthew sets what for him is the most important statement to be made about God at the very beginning of his gospel: In this Jesus is revealed the God who liberates and chooses as well as the one who pardons and forgives sins; it is this God who causes God's new covenant to dawn in Jesus.

Incarnate as a Jew

Matthew, in recalling the reconciling and forgiving God through the weeping of Rachel, leads us deep into the meaning of the new covenant. The children of Bethlehem could not go on living; they could not give their names to children and grandchildren as a memorial. The children of Bethlehem require a memorial sign, Yad Vashem, and Matthew gives it to them in order to remind Christians of all ages, at the beginning of the good news of the new covenant, of their beginning and origin in the people Israel.

Would the Holocaust, the Shoah, *the* human catastrophe, have been possible if we Christian had recalled, every Christmas, that God not only became a human being, but a *Jew?* If we had taken Matthew's Christmas message seriously, in the way in which it roots us Christians in Israel, would we have been spared from having to recognize and experience Auschwitz as "an attack on everything that should have been sacred to Christians as well" (Johannes Baptist Metz)? Would there have been a Shoah in our land if we had given the children of Bethlehem their Yad Vashem?

In light of this, does not the ever-recurring prayer in the Jewish liturgy for the Day of Atonement belong in the "festival of our redemption" as well?

"O God, pardon us, forgive us, reconcile us!"

You, Bethlehem . . .

Year after year, with professional routine, the cameras of the international television crews are trained on the little town south of Jerusalem and send their pictures, from the shepherds' field to the Grotto of the Nativity, by the million around the world. It is Christmas, the Holy Night, and through the cameras the whole world looks to Bethlehem. Once a year this little place becomes the center of the world. Is this not a fulfillment of what was written by the prophet Micah in the Old Testament?

> But you, O Bethlehem of Ephrathah,
>> who are one of the little clans of Judah,
> from you shall come forth for me
>> one who is to rule in Israel,
> whose origin is from of old,
>> from ancient days. (Mic 5:2)

This verse is well known to us on the tongues of the scribes and high priests whom King Herod questions after the Wise Men from the East have come to him and asked about the newborn king of the Jews (Matthew 2). This is a prophetic word that— through the prophets—is a word received from God. God in person speaks to this tiny village, just as God had spoken to Jerusalem through the prophet Micah, shortly before:

> And you, O tower of the flock,
>> hill of daughter Zion,
> to you it shall come,
>> the former dominion shall come,
> the sovereignty of daughter Jerusalem. (Mic 4:8)

The contrast can scarcely be greater: here the major city, the center of Israel, and there the little, insignificant village. But God never contrasts the two. This passage is neither about the importance of the holy city nor about preference for the smaller. Instead, the word of God places the two side by side and allows the unique and special character of each to stand out. It reminds us a little of the tribal ancestor Jacob, who at the end of his life calls his sons together and blesses them by naming what is characteristic of each as descriptive of his destiny (cf. Genesis 49). In these words past and future flow together. The future, including what is promised, whether it is the future of Jacob's sons, Israel's tribes, or Jerusalem and Bethlehem, cannot be separated from what came before.

God Amazes

Promise and blessing have deep roots, no longer visible in what comes to be, but still necessary for life. Only those who seek the roots will understand and experience the depth of promise and blessing. For Israel the roots of the holy city, Jerusalem, go only back to King David. He conquered the city, made it *his* city, the city of David. In place of the dwelling that David wanted to build for God, a temple in Jerusalem, God promises him an immortal house, an everlasting dynasty (2 Samuel 7). But David's successors on the throne in Jerusalem soon forgot what had united David and God. They went their own ways and claimed to be the sons of David whom God had promised to stand by and uphold.

But God's ways are not only unfathomable; above all, they are incalculable for human beings. God amazes us because God causes the unexpected to happen—the unexpected thing that then proves to be the most deep-seated consequence, and not a matter of caprice. Thus God, through the prophet Isaiah, can proclaim even to the Davidic dynasty, who counted on their pedigree:

> A shoot shall come out from the stump of Jesse,
>> and a branch shall grow out of his roots.
> The spirit of the LORD shall rest on him,
>> the spirit of wisdom and understanding,

the spirit of counsel and might,
the spirit of knowledge and the fear of the LORD. (Isa 11:1-2)

This image—sugared and made toothless in Christmas carols—is clear and unmistakable, and its severity is practically unsurpassable. The family tree of the Davidides is struck down, and yet God remains true to the promise—but in a way that is humanly incalculable. God returns to the point at which God's history with David began, to David's father Jesse. That is the hidden root of David, his election. Through the prophet Samuel, God had anointed the youngest of Jesse's sons (1 Samuel 16).

Forgotten Beginning?

God, in order to realize the goal planned for humankind, returns to the beginning, to the place we have long forgotten because we have allowed such great things to come to be alongside it, mighty and noteworthy things. This place to which God returns in order to carry out the promises is Bethlehem! Bethlehem is not, first of all, David's city; no, David's city is Jerusalem. Bethlehem is the town of Jesse, David's father, the town of the roots: tiny, unnoticed, almost forgotten alongside Jerusalem.

For the prophet Micah and many other biblical traditions Bethlehem became a symbol of the power of the roots with which anyone who wants to grow in faith must remain connected. Bethlehem is the place of God's free election against all human calculation and assurance. However, Bethlehem is no longer the village idyll of shepherds and farmers; it is the place of the Messiah, the place of salvation. Bethlehem warns us that God's salvation is not u-topia, not placeless, but is solidly anchored in our world: in Bethlehem.

Bethlehem: The Root of Faith

As the place of Jesus' birth, Bethlehem draws us Christians to the roots of our faith. Bethlehem confronts us seriously with God's history and God's promises, which are not fulfilled by being ended, closed, and falling due, but by the fact that God confirms them as promises. That is what Bethlehem stands for, that and God's faithfulness even and especially when something entirely new seems to be beginning. Then Bethlehem, which we so often speak about and sing about at Christmas, can be a sign for us to think of the roots of Christianity in the Old Testament. This is not about the "root of Jesse," the motif of direct and uniform connection between Old and New Testament that Christian art has developed for us over the centuries, out of David's origins, in an infinite variety of forms; it is rather about the root of which Paul reminds us:

> . . . if the root is holy, then the branches also are holy. But if some of the branches were broken off, and you, a wild olive shoot, were grafted in their place to share the rich root of the olive tree, do not boast over the branches. If you do boast, remember that it is not you that support the root, but the root that supports you. (Rom 11:16-18)

The messianic hope that is found in the text from Isaiah that speaks of the new shoot from the root of Jesse goes back to those roots to indicate the depth of the connection. The artist Sieger Köder sensed that connection and depicted the double motif of origins in his picture, "Bethlehem-Ephratah, from you one will come forth," found on the cover of this book: Bethlehem as Jesse's place (Micah 5) and the new shoot from Jesse's roots (Isaiah 11).

Advent in Bethlehem

When we Christians at Christmastide hear about Bethlehem, see Bethlehem, and surround Bethlehem with Christmas music it can be a wonderful sign for us that we must be on the way. This Christmas route leads to a goal beyond the manger, for the place where that manger stands points like a signpost to a long prior history with its origins in days long ago, as the prophet Micah emphasizes in the text quoted: ". . . whose origin is from of old, from ancient days" (Mic 5:2). Our faith can only live out of its origins, and this origin of ours is in Israel, in the people of God, in Bethlehem. . . .

When we surrender ourselves to the depths of our faith in the Old Testament we will also be strengthened, for we will find rich and filling nourishment here. Is it accidental that Bethlehem, literally translated, means "house of bread"?

Bethlehem, you are so small and have so much to tell us!

Bethlehem is the trace of Christmas in the Old Testament—
or better: a trace that leads us into the Old Testament, not only at
Christmas. Thus may Advent become reality, a coming to Bethlehem and a coming to ourselves as Christians. A sign of this, more
than all the Christmas images from the television cameras, are the
Christians from Jerusalem who every year, in the holy night, set
out on foot to go to Bethlehem.

Following the Traces

The track that draws us from the Christmas message of the New Testament deep into the Old Testament, the trace that has been pursued by the reflections in this book, has already been followed, and not only by individual Christians: the Church's liturgy (sometimes in ways more hidden than apparent) has preserved many elements of it.

At the beginning of the book we pointed to the special character of Advent, which was not always a time of preparation for Christmas, but instead closed the Church year, while Christmas, with its remembrance of the Incarnation, began a new year. Over a long period of time the liturgy built up this aspect of "beginning" through the Christmas season in order to make the manifold character of this feast live for the people in its celebrations. After the focal celebration of the Incarnation on Christmas itself, particular features of the Savior as God and human being were commemorated in special feasts. The octave of Christmas, January 1, was celebrated as the feast of the Circumcision of the Lord to give expression to the fact that the divine incarnation took place in concrete form, that God came to God's people: that is, that the incarnation of God also meant God's becoming a Jew. The feast balancing this "human side" was Epiphany on January 6, making visible and honoring the divine character of the newborn child. In this perspective the feasts of the Circumcision and Epiphany constitute a wonderful unit that develops the theme of Christmas in light of its christology: God and human being. But that unity was deeply disturbed when, in 1960, the name of the feast of the Circumcision of the Lord was eliminated; in 1969 it was entirely replaced by the Solemnity of Mary, the Mother of God, now occurring on the octave of Christmas.

Was it intended that in this way the concretion of the incarnation of God in Jesus of Nazareth's birth as a Jew should be forgotten? Was there a deliberate effort to destroy what Paul so clearly emphasized in Gal 4:4: "But when the fullness of time had come, God sent his Son, born of a woman, born under the law"?

We can only speculate on the causes for the elimination of this feast, since no clarification was offered. But it was surely more than the brief statement in Luke that was read as the Gospel on the feast of the Circumcision that was lost to the consciousness of believers with and through the abolition of the feast: "After eight days had passed, it was time to circumcise the child; and he was called Jesus, the name given by the angel before he was conceived in the womb" (Luke 2:21).

Did we not also forget, in this way, that our Christian roots are in Judaism, and that the New Testament itself repeatedly recalls that the salvation of the world enduringly involves the Jews? When Jesus himself emphatically says in John's gospel, "Salvation is [not "comes," as it is frequently translated!] from the Jews" (John 4:22) "can Christians ever afford to forget it? If Christianity had never forgotten it, perhaps theological antisemitism and its dreadful consequences would have been impossible. Statements have consequences!" writes the important New Testament scholar and inaugural figure in Jewish-Christian dialogue, Franz Mußner. Statements have consequences, even forgotten statements, even forgotten and abolished feastdays! When in our days, in connection with the Vatican document on the destruction of the Jews, the Shoah, the Pope appeals to us: "Remember: Jesus was a Jew," then we should ask in turn whether it may be that such a reminder is so urgently necessary because the feast that uniquely recalls it has been suppressed. Much has been said and written in the Church in recent years about the Jewish woman Edith Stein, now canonized. When she converted to Christianity she deliberately chose as the day of her baptism the feast of Jesus' circumcision. That should do more than make us reflect on the abolished and forgotten feast.

Profound Traces in Prayer

The antiphons for the feast of the Circumcision can still be found in the liturgy of the hours at Evening Prayer II on the octave of Christmas. They adopt Old Testament motifs traditionally associated with the feast of Christmas (and discussed in the chapters above):

First Antiphon: "O marvelous exchange! The creator of humanity has become a human being, born of a virgin. Begotten by no man, he comes into the world and bestows divine life on us."

Second Antiphon: "O unspeakably deep mystery! By your miraculous birth of the Virgin you have fulfilled the Scriptures: like a gentle rain falling upon the earth you have come down to save your people. O God, we praise you."

Third Antiphon: "O burning bush that Moses saw! Flaming, you did not burn. In you we see the likeness of the blessed Virgin, who bore unblemished. Pray for us, Mother of God."[1]

In their form, beginning with the acclamation "O," these antiphons correspond to the great "O" antiphons of the seven liturgical days from December 16–22, which in turn brightly illuminate the Old Testament roots of the Christmas message, and so point to the traces we have been following in this book.

December 16: "O Wisdom, you came forth from the mouth of the Most High and reach from one end of the earth to the other, mightily and sweetly ordering all things. O come and teach us the way of prudence."

December 17: "O Adonai and Leader of the house of Israel, you appeared to Moses in the fire of the burning bush and gave him the law on Sinai. O come and redeem us with an outstretched arm."

December 18: "O Root of Jesse, you stand as an ensign to the peoples; before you kings will shut their mouths and nations will bow in worship. O come and deliver us and do not tarry."

December 19: "O Key of David and Scepter of the house of Israel, you open and no one can close; you close and no one can

---

[1] The antiphons are here translated from the author's German text.

open. O come and bring captives out of the prison house, those who sit in darkness and the shadow of death."

December 20: "O Rising Dawn, brightness of the Light Eternal and Sun of Righteousness, O come and enlighten those who sit in darkness and the shadow of death."

December 21: "O King of the Nations and the Desire of them all, you are the Cornerstone who makes both one. O come and save the creatures whom you fashioned out of clay."

December 22: "O Emmanuel, our King and Lawgiver, the Expected of the nations and the Savior of them all, O come and save us, O Lord our God."

When the octave before Christmas is so exalted by these ideas and formulae in the "O" antiphons, drawn from the Old Testament, and especially from the book of Isaiah, it is by no means least for the purpose of drawing our attention and sharpening our senses for the octave-day after Christmas, which, in the feast of the Circumcision of the Lord, extends the sense of this deep rootedness in the Old Testament, and hence the unbreakable connection between Judaism and Christianity.

Like the Magi who followed the star, we can also follow, in the liturgy of Advent and Christmas, the traces that lead us into the Old Testament. Following that track, we can arrive at the place from which we came, at the origin of our Christianity, so that we can really become Advent Christians, as described at the beginning of this book, for it is true of us as Christians that

It all began before Christmas!